T0179397

Emerging Trends in Disruptive Technology Management for Sustainable Development

Chapman & Hall/CRC
Computational Intelligence
and Its Applications

Series Editor: Siddhartha Bhattacharyya

Intelligent Copyright Protection for Images
Subhrajit Sinha Roy, Abhishek Basu, Avik Chattopadhyay

Emerging Trends in Disruptive Technology Management for Sustainable Development
Rik Das, Mahua Banerjee, Sourav De

For more information about this series please visit:
https://www.crcpress.com/Chapman--HallCRC-Computational-Intelligence-and-Its-Applications/book-series/CIAFOCUS

Emerging Trends in Disruptive Technology Management for Sustainable Development

Edited by
Rik Das, Mahua Banerjee,
and Sourav De

CRC Press
Taylor & Francis Group
Boca Raton London New York

CRC Press is an imprint of the
Taylor & Francis Group, an **informa** business
A CHAPMAN & HALL BOOK

CRC Press
Taylor & Francis Group
52 Vanderbilt Avenue
New York, NY 10017

© 2020 by Taylor & Francis Group, LLC
CRC Press is an imprint of Taylor & Francis Group, an Informa business

No claim to original U.S. Government works

Printed on acid-free paper

International Standard Book Number-13: 978-0-367-24964-9 (Hardback)

Rik Das would like to dedicate this book to his father, Mr. Kamal Kumar Das, his mother, Mrs. Malabika Das, his better half, Mrs. Simi Das, and his kids, Sohan and Dikshan

Mahua Banerjee would like to dedicate this book to his father, Amala Kanta Mukherjee, and Rita Mukherjee

Sourav De would like to dedicate this book to his loving wife, Debolina, beloved son, Aishik, and grandmother, Late Kamalabala De

CONTENTS

PREFACE

Researchers and professionals are fascinated time and again by applications of technology in management practices. Different technical innovations create significant impacts in daily managerial operations. Recent developments in disruptive technologies, like machine learning, deep learning, blockchain, etc. have soared to newer heights in gaining competitive advantages for business. The Internet of Things (IoT) has changed the daily lives of the masses and has created prominent business values for the business houses. It has literally portrayed the effectiveness of interdisciplinary applications and has identified novel horizons in the area of technology management. Applications like blockchain have ensured one-stop cryptographic solutions to business transactions. The immense data produced due to the technical advancements are useful to create valuable insights into consumer behaviour with the help of big data analysis. In this context, machine learning and computer vision play a huge role in bringing the technocrats and management graduates under the same roof for decision-making and execution. Thus, there is an enormous obligation to highlight the fusion of technology and management to leverage the mammoth power of interdisciplinary research for scientists, scholars, entrepreneurs, and business houses for designing a better tomorrow and a sustainable world to live in.

This volume has collated a broad spectrum of artificial intelligence applications under the purview of sustainable development and management practices so that it is able to trigger further inspiration among various research communities to contribute in their respective fields of applications, thereby orienting these application fields toward techno-managerial research and development.

The first chapter has proposed IoT-based techniques for plant stress identification to promote sustainable agriculture. Plant stress in the agriculture field not only hampers the quality of agricultural production but also reduces the quantity. The generated data from the IoT platform can be fed into an intelligent system for processing the data to detect plant stresses, which in turn helps the farmer to decide on the pesticides.

The second chapter has analyzed the achievability of sustainable development goals (SDGs) by means of IoT. The major SDGs include good health, clean water and sanitation, gender equality, climate action, clean energy, and sustainable cities. The "Internet of Things" is a modern sensing, signalling, controlling, and communication technology that is poised to play a significant role in improving all the above-mentioned goals for sustainability.

Smartphone crowd computing is a promising research domain emphasized in the third chapter. Extensive usage of e-devices and gadgets with quite low use cycles churns out a huge amount of not-easy-to-decompose e-waste. This has tremendous negative effect on Earth's environment as well as on living beings. The primary aim of this chapter is to eliminate the environmental externalities of the existing computing systems and provide an alternative sustainable solution in order to minimise the environmental hazards.

Finally, the fourth chapter has presented a study on marine life engineering. It has used Computational Fluid Dynamics (CFD) simulators such as SOLEIL and BhT to study the shape and size of real-time fish, which can be incorporated into the design aspects of robotic fish. Usage of shape-memory alloys (SMAs) leading to compact design and minimized energy consumption along with flexible materials used to design a tail fin section to achieve maximum efficiency is discussed in this chapter; improving overall swimming performance of carangiform and ostraciform modes through relevant and possible key characteristics of fish is also discussed.

This volume has attempted the assembling of diverse research communities in a single platform to ventilate their ideas in a more structured manner. The present endeavour may be seen as the inception of efforts to bring interdisciplinary research ideas and applications across complementary fields of techno-managerial interpretation and analysis into close proximity.

Dr. Rik Das

Dr. Mahua Banerjee

Dr. Sourav De

MATLAB® is a registered trademark of The MathWorks, Inc. For product information, please contact:

The MathWorks, Inc.
3 Apple Hill Drive
Natick, MA 01760-2098 USA
Tel: 508 647 7000
Fax: 508-647-7001
E-mail: info@mathworks.com
Web: www.mathworks.com

EDITORS

 Dr. Rik Das has pursued a broad range of research interests in the domain of machine learning and deep learning applications for content-based image identification. He is an Assistant Professor in the Department of Information Technology, Xavier Institute of Social Service, Ranchi, Jharkhand, India.

Dr. Das earned a Ph.D. from the University of Calcutta, India, and pursued his M.Tech in Information Technology from the same university. He earned his B.E. in Information Technology from the University of Burdwan, India. His research spans multiple interdisciplinary approaches and has won accolades in the research community for manifold applications.

Dr. Das has more than 10 years of research experience and 16 years of teaching experience. He has 24 international publications to date with reputed publishers, namely, IEEE, Springer, Emerald, Inderscience, and so on. He is a reviewer for leading journals, such as, *Journal of Visual Communication and Image Representation*, Elsevier, *Transactions on Mutimedia*, IEEE, *LNCS Transactions on Computational Science*, Springer, etc. He has carried out collaborative research work with institutions in India and abroad. He frequently delivers invited sessions on artificial intelligence and machine learning in industry and academia. He has also chaired sessions at *International Conferences on Image Processing* and has acted as a resource person in refresher courses on information technology. He is associated as a Ph.D. supervisor with reputed universities and is guiding multiple Ph.D. scholars for quality research output.

Dr. Das is always open to discuss new research ideas for collaborative research work and for techno-managerial consultancies.

Dr. Mahua Banerjee heads the Department of Information Technology, Xavier Institute of Social Service, Ranchi. Jharkhand, India. She graduated from Bethune College, Kolkata, India, in Physics (Honours). She earned her Post graduate Diploma in Computer Application (PGDCA) from the Xavier Institute of Social Service and a Master's in Computer Application from Indira Gandhi National Open University (IGNOU). Thereafter she completed her Ph.D. in Computer Science from the Indian School of Mines (IIT), Dhanbad. Her research area was in software engineering.

Since 1990, she has been teaching postgraduate students in different topics like procedure-oriented programming, object-oriented programming, database management systems, data structure and algorithm, data communication and networking, operations and production management, etc. She has around 11 national and international publications in journals and proceedings. She has also authored books on modular programming with reputed international publishers. She has reviewed several books in C and C++ programming, Data structure algorithm and data communication networking, McGraw Hill Publication. Her research interests include software engineering and modular programming.

Dr. Sourav De earned his Bachelor's in Information Technology from the University of Burdwan, Burdwan, India, in 2002. He earned his Master's in Information Technology from the West Bengal University of Technology, Kolkata, India, in 2005. He completed his Ph.D. in Computer Science and Technology from the Indian Institute of Engineering and Technology, Shibpur, Howrah, India, in 2015. He is currently an Associate Professor in the Computer Science and Engineering Department in Cooch Behar Government Engineering College, West Bengal, India. Prior to this, he was an Assistant Professor for more than 10 years in the Department of Computer Science and Engineering and Information Technology of University

Institute of Technology, the University of Burdwan, Burdwan, India. He served as a Junior Programmer in Apices Consultancy Private Limited, Kolkata, India, in 2005. He is a co-author of one book and the co-editor of six books and has more than 38 research publications in internationally reputed journals, international edited books, and international IEEE conference proceedings; he also has one patent to his credit. He served as a reviewer in several international IEEE conferences and also in several international editorial books. He also served as a reviewer in some reputed international journals, such as *Applied Soft Computing*, Elsevier, *Knowledge-Based Systems, Computer Methods in Biomechanics and Biomedical Engineering: Imaging & Visualization, Inderscience Journals*, etc. He has been the member of the organizing and technical program committees of several national and international conferences. He has been invited to different seminars as an expert speaker. His research interests include soft computing, pattern recognition, image processing, and data mining. Dr. De is a member of IEEE, ACM, Computer Science Teachers Association (CSTA), Institute of Engineers and International Association of Engineers (IAENG), Hong Kong. He is a life member of ISTE, India.

CONTRIBUTORS

Sudip Chatterjee
Amity School of Engineering
   and Technology
Amity University
West Bengal, India

Prasenjit Choudhury
National Institute of Technology
West Bengal, India

Vikram Kulkarni
Department of Information
   Technology
Mukesh Patel School of
   Technology Management and
   Engineering
Mumbai, India

Rejo Mathew
Mukesh Patel School of
   Technology Management &
   Engineering
Mumbai, India

Debarshi Mazumder
Budge Budge Institute of
   Technology
West Bengal, India

Sudarshan Nandy
Amity School of Engineering
   and Technology
Amity University
West Bengal, India

Adetan Oluwumi
Ekiti State University
Ado Ekiti, Nigeria

Saurabh Pal
Bengal Institute of Technology
West Bengal, India

Pijush Kanti Dutta Pramanik
National Institute of Technology
West Bengal, India

S. Raja Mohamed
Kalaignarkarunanidhi Institute
   of Technology
Tamil Nadu, India

P. Raviraj
GSSSITEW Institute
   of Engineering and
   Technology
Karnataka, India

1

IoT-BASED INTELLIGENT SYSTEM FOR IDENTIFICATION OF PLANT STRESS IN SUSTAINABLE AGRICULTURE

Debarshi Mazumder, Sudarshan Nandy, and Sudip Chatterjee

CONTENTS

1.1 INTRODUCTION

The increasing global population demands quality food while maintaining the food quantity and the environment. It is estimated that the global population will be approximately 9 billion by 2050 and hence food production should increase by 70 per cent [1]. In developed and underdeveloped countries, the demand for the food is completed from agriculture-based products. Sustainable agriculture has a remarkable prospect in the field of agricultural production to fulfil the food requirements of the global population by maintaining the environmental ecology. In sustainable agriculture, advanced technologies are incorporated to detect plant stress, which has a direct impact on the quality and quantity of the agriculture product [2]. The growth of a plant in an unsatisfactory environment may be the cause behind the plant stresses. The effects of stresses can lead to deficiencies in growth, permanent damage, or death of plant; this reduces the quality as well as the quantity of the food production [3]. Plant stress factors are generally divided into two sets: biotic (includes living biological factors such as fungi, bacteria, virus, insects, parasites, weeds, etc.) and abiotic (includes non-living environmental factors such as light, water, temperature, drought, flood, nutrient deficiency, and other environmental factors) [4, 5]. In agriculture, environmental and biological factors play an important role in the growth, development, and productivity of the plant. Every plant gives good productivity if stress factors are within appropriate limits. Any unexpected changes in environmental and biological factors can cause deficiencies or damages in plant productivity and these changes may affect several parts of the plant, such as root, leaf, etc. [6]. It is observed that every biotic and abiotic stress consists of threshold values for the plant, and under this threshold value, good productivity can be expected [3, 7]. These unexpected or critical changes in the environmental or biological factors can exceed the threshold levels and it is then the main cause behind the deficiencies in productivity [8]. Usually, the identification and monitoring of the plant stresses are done by farmers with the naked eye, but nowadays detection of plant stresses due to biotic factors is also done using an Internet of Things (IoT)-based intelligent system [9, 10]. In this respect, IoT-based intelligent systems in sustainable agriculture is the most significant way to identify plant stresses as quickly as possible, and it is possible to decide correct and accurate amount of pesticide or another remedy [11–13].

Currently, IoT intelligent systems are used widely in the agricultural domain. Advancement and existing challenges present in IoT will make it more popular in the future [1]. An IoT-based intelligent system performs the commendable job of continuous monitoring in the concerned agriculture field and making predictions and decisions regarding the plant stresses of the field [14]. This advanced system has collected the raw data or information from numerous disparate systems. As per system requirements, these data are processed, segmented, and systematized by some smart algorithms [15]. In another process, some advanced algorithms are applied in agriculture for analyzing the data to identify and detect the early threats or warnings that are produced by the IoT-based prediction system [16]. If a system generates any threat or warning, then an alert is created automatically and an appropriate solution or remedy is suggested to the agriculture field-monitoring objects such as farmer, agriculture robot, agriculture vehicle, etc [17]. An IoT-based intelligent system is cost-effective because it works on low power and stores the data into distributed databases. Further, analyzed or processed overheads by these systems are effortlessly transferred to the cloud, where more devices are connected in a distributed manner, and, thus, computational speed is increased [1, 18].

In the agriculture field, identification and monitoring of plant stresses with the naked eye is very tedious and leads to low-quality, insufficient production. For this reason, the IoT-based intelligent system is introduced to sustainable agriculture to detect or identify the plant stress. The survey of this chapter covers the IoT-based hybrid intelligent techniques which help to identify, detect, or predict the plant stress in agriculture production. The other objective of this survey is to perform a comparative study on different machine learning (ML) methods which helps to observe and analyze different plant stress parameters. The rest of this survey is organized through the discussion of IOT and intelligent system techniques for processing an object. First, the survey concentrates on the IoT structure and its detail layer-based discussion. In Section 1.3, methodology to perform this survey is described. The sub-section consists of the machine learning process for agriculture with a detailed view of each phase of data processing. Section 1.4 depicts the importance of IoT based intelligent system for plant stress detection. Finally, the survey concludes with the future scope.

1.2 ORGANIZATION OF IoT

The Internet of Things is an extremely favourable hybrid technological system in the present world that provides various activities like sensing, monitoring, controlling, actuating, etc [19–21]. It is represented through physical and virtual systems, which are interconnected with the internet. Data are collected in the IoT systems from numerous objects like physical devices and transferred to the server instances through high-speed internet. The virtual system or instances of cloud performs various computational analysis on these data to create appropriate decisions. In IoT, each device either physically or virtually is connected to the system is known as "Things." Examples of these physical devices are digital cameras, numerous sensors, etc. The virtual system or resources in the cloud service help us with its machine learning services. These services are basically associated with a user application from which the user may get the required information [22–25]. In this study, Figure 1.1 represents a layer structure of IoT for agriculture systems. The layers are perception or sensing layer, data transfer or network layer, and data storage and manipulation layer or application layer. In the perception layer, data are collected from various near-field sources like cameras and sensors or sensor-based devices. Image-based data are also collected or fed into the perception layer like weather station data, historical data, statistical reports, etc. In the network layer, these data are transferred to the database instance of the cloud system via numerous network devices and gateways. In the final layer, all system intelligence techniques are applied, with high computation and decision-making taking place [1, 15, 17, 19, 23].

> **Layer 1: Perception Layer**—In the agriculture sector, this layer consists of numerous sensors and cameras. Different types of sensors and cameras are collecting various types of raw data from the agriculture field. Agriculture field sensors are collecting data related to humidity, temperature, intensity of light, nitrogen concentration, soil moisture, etc. [26–30]. On the other side, cameras are capturing image-based data. These images

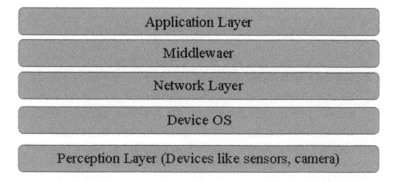

Figure 1.1 Layered structure of IoT.

are injuries or affected regions of the plant (stem, root, leaf, etc.), the image of plant diseases, pest or insect attacks, fungal infections, etc. [31–37].

Layer 2: Network Layer—In this layer, IoT devices or nodes indirectly or directly send the raw data to the application hosted on the cloud-based platform by communicating with each other over a gateway [16, 19]. Devices are connected to each other through wired or wireless communication. Mostly, wireless sensor network (WSN) is used for communication [38]. Naturally, devices in a wireless sensor network involve a module that can be used for processing tasks, operating with minimum power. Commonly, the WSN module includes a microcontroller unit (MCU), single or multiple sensor devices connected externally or internally and a radio frequency (RF)-based communication node [39, 40].

Layer 3: Application Layer—This is the most important layer in the structure of IoT. It offers different types of software-based application components that store, collect, monitor, and perform the computational tasks in various parts of IoT [1, 16]. At the very beginning stage, one common challenge is to recognize each device uniquely. The uniqueness of a device is represented in various ways, such as reliability, identity, scalability, and persistence [22, 24]. The consequent big challenge in this layer is pre-processing and organizing the raw data that can be suitable for acceptance by the analyzing or decision-making applications [1, 16]. Several image-processing methodologies (such as pre-processing, resizing, and segmentation) for images and data validation techniques for sensors data are used to prepare the data perfectly and can be incorporated in appropriate applications [34, 41–45]. One central application exists in every application layer of IoT that accepts all the processed data from numerous application present in this layer or sub-layers. In this application, data are processed, analyzed, and classified through various intelligent algorithms which help to predict and detect any plant stress [46]. Machine learning- or deep learning-based algorithms are widely used in this layer. The main reasons for choosing machine learning, or one of the biggest advantages of ML, is the ability to solve a large number of datasets independently, including linear and non-linear problems [47, 48].

1.2.1 An Organized View of the Overall System

The architectural view of the overall system is depicted in Figure 1.2. This phase of the survey discusses the association of the IoT with machine learning and its possibility in the agricultural process development. The primary elements of the IoT, i.e., camera, sensor, or other devices, feed the data to the IoT layer. The raw data is then shared with the server instances in the cloud for its pre-processing. The preprocessing methods in the cloud incorporate different techniques to remove the unwanted noise and sample it at a constant rate. The feature extraction algorithms are applied over that sample to analyze the data. These features are prepared a dataset and then it is considered in any machine learning algorithm for prediction and detection on the plant stress. Once analyzed and detected, that information is again synchronized to an IoT device which updates the cloud instance where the application is hosted. This application is the end point of the system that users are logged into. So, the farmer is updated with possible detection of plant stress through that application.

The key goal of this IoT-based intelligent system in sustainable agriculture is to improve the agriculture productivity and quality through detection of plant stress with minimum human effort, and it also helps us to minimize the cost of operation [49]. The prospective growth of development in quality and improvement in productivity is determined by various dissimilar production elements. These elements are weather conditions (which includes humidity, the intensity

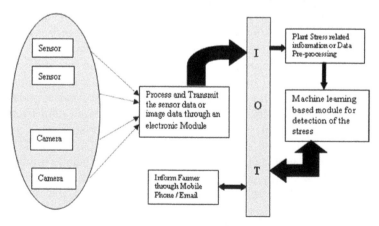

Figure 1.2 The architecture of the IoT-based intelligent system for sustainable agriculture.

of sunlight, temperature, wind speed, etc.), soil properties, nutrient status, pest or disease management, weed management, landscape management, irrigation, and fertilizer management [50–52]. These elements are important for agricultural productivity, and disturbance in any one of the elements hampers the plant health and its proper growth. For this reason, an IoT-based intelligent system is essential for agriculture-based plant health monitoring and controlling. If any stress exists in plant or agricultural environments, IoT-based intelligent systems automatically detect and forecast it to the farmer or agriculture robot or vehicle and provide a suitable solution or remedy with or without human interferences [53, 54].

1.3 METHODOLOGY

In this section, the different phases' article collection process is explained in detail. The survey of this chapter is evolved through the following stages: (a) gathering of correlated works, (b) refining of appropriate works, and (c) comprehensive assessment and analysis of these works. In the initial step, some keywords are used for searching for conference papers, journals, books articles, etc. These keywords are "Plant Stress" AND ["Internet of Things" OR "Intelligent System"] AND "Sustainable Agriculture" AND ["Machine Learning" OR "Deep Learning"]. By using this keyword-based searching, papers are collected over plant stress, IoT-based sustainable agriculture, and machine learning topics. In this step, authors also try to strain out those papers that are not referring to the agriculture or IoT domain. Standing assessments or surveys were also perused for interconnected work. From this scuffle, 132 papers were primarily recognized from the relevant fields. In the subsequent step, looking on to the important factors presented by the papers or articles, 80 papers are finalized for the study. It is also checked whether these papers actually involve the use of IoT or machine learning in plant stress detection or not. In the final step, the carefully chosen papers from the previous step were analyzed one-by-one, considering or identifying the issues. The issues in these papers have tried to focus on difficulties addressed, the resolution proposed, impact reached (if measurable), tools used, systems and algorithms used, foundations of data engaged in IoT and machine learning techniques.

In this section, an IoT-based intelligent system is described with a detailed discussion on data processing and machine learning (Figure 1.3). This model is derived and designed by considering the

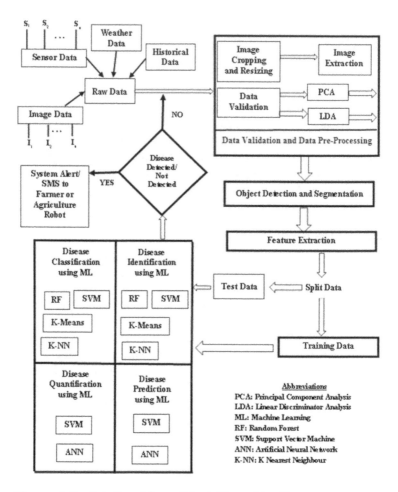

Figure 1.3   Detail workflow of the IoT-based intelligent system.

subsequent developments of IoT and machine learning for the agricultural system. In various relevant literature, different components of the figure were partially developed to monitor the plant in an agricultural field. Here, in this proposed model, all the components are put together to understand the IoT-based intelligent system model. According to Figure 1.3 the main components of this systems are (1) data collection, (2) data pre-processing and data validation, (3) object detection or segmentation, (4) feature extraction, (5) classification and identification or prediction, (6) solution or remedy informed.

1.3.1 Data Collection

In the initial stage, numerous agriculture data from various sources are collected. Data are of two types: either sensor-based, image-based, or both. Apart from these, some historical and statistical data are also used in the data collection stage. Together, all the types of data are known as "raw data". These raw data are fed to the IoT-based system automatically. Sensor-based data are captured through numerous sensors that are deployed in the agriculture field and weather station. Image-based data are captured through the farmer's mobile or camera, satellites, or drones and cameras deployed in the agriculture field [55–57, 60]. After collecting, these raw data need to transfer to local databases or local cloud for further processing. These raw data are not directly acceptable by the central intelligent system due to various causes. First, captured images are not suitable for work due to the improper size, image celerity, or wrong inputs. On the other side, sensor-based data can lead to inconsistent or wrong input due to high humidity, high temperature, heavy rainfall, or snowfall. For this reason, raw data from the data collection stage requires data validation and pre-processing, where it is identified and processed further in an appropriate format [58–62].

1.3.2 Data Validation and Pre-Processing

In this process, various image-processing methodologies are used for data validation and pre-processing. For Images, pre-processing techniques are image cropping, image resizing, and image extraction. Image cropping is a methodology by which unessential or unwanted sections are removed from raw images. Image resizing is also required because images are captured from different angles and sizes. Image resizing is fixing the total number of pixels' size and rotating or distorting an image. Image extracting is the method to remove undesirable objects from images [34, 63, 64]. On another side, sensor-based data are also needed to be validated and pre-processed through some validation and pre-processing techniques for better acquisition and computing. In some studies, authors incorporate principal component analysis (PCA) and linear discriminator analysis (LCA) methodologies for data validation and pre-processing [47].

1.3.3 Object Detection and Segmentation

Object detection represents identifying or finding the location of an object in an image depending on certain features. Image segmentation is the process of dividing an image into multiple images based on certain characteristics such as shape, colour, or texture. Sensor-based data also can be segregated and divided depending on multiple blocks or segments based on their properties or attributes. The aim of image or data segmentation is to make simpler and/or modify the representation of an image or data in such a way that it is more significant and stress-free to analyze [65–68, 79].

1.3.4 Feature Extraction

Feature extraction is a method to study the previously processed data from its original set. The purpose of this study is to construct or transform original set into manageable groups or set of values based on some properties that can sufficiently identify an object uniquely [69, 70]. The feature groups or set of feature values are still precisely and entirely representing the original data set of an object or image. Depending on the computational techniques or methodology, further, these feature sets can be divided into two parts, such as training dataset and test dataset. The end of the feature extraction process, feature sets are ready to include in a central intelligent system [71, 72, 76].

1.3.5 Machine Learning Methods

Machine learning is a multidisciplinary technique that borrows heavily from probability theory, statistics, decision theory, visualization, and optimization. Machine learning can handle a very large amount of data, including image datasets, to provide analytical outputs. The machine learning is consists of stages such as pre-processing (segmentation, clustering); identification or detection; and, lastly, prediction. A large portion of the dataset is selected for the "training" of the system, so that subset is called "training dataset." This dataset is actually calibrating the system. The rest portion of the dataset is left as "testing dataset." The IoT-based intelligent system presented in Figure 1.3 is a supervised model. The first criterion of supervision is the labelling of training image data. Labelling is done by specifying the species of the plant of an image. If the label is not provided, then it is an unsupervised model. The intelligent system is represented as a single unit that consists of one single or a collection of machine learning algorithms. These algorithms perform various computation on the feature sets [73, 74]. These algorithms are able to predict, identify or detect, classify, and quantify the stress of an agriculture field.

In Figure 1.3, the support vector machines (SVM) and regular artificial neural networks (ANN) are popular examples of supervised schemes. ANN is the backbone of this machine learning system used in this IoT-based system. Unsupervised learning finds some specific structures or features present in the plant images. Unsupervised learning identifies tassels or pods or other features. So, once the supervised or unsupervised prediction or identification of plant stress is countable, the system sends an auto-generated alert to the farmer, agriculture robot, or actuators deployed in the agriculture field. Depending on the issues, a proper remedy or solution is also made available to the farmer through the IoT-based intelligent system [75–80].

1.4 DISCUSSION

Plant stresses are the most common reason for unsatisfactory agricultural production. To raise agricultural production, it is of uncountable implication in the monitoring, recognizing, and controlling of agricultural stresses with advanced technology. Presently, agronomic organization accountabilities through computer visualization are enticing a hot research zone supportive in noticeable indications identification on the plant. Enormous varieties of problems linked to farming are currently shared by the methods of IoT and predicted by the machine learning techniques. The IoT-based intelligent model in Figure 1.3 is communicated with numerous devices or systems, which are interconnected through the high-speed network system. IoT-based intelligent system is engaging different algorithms, methods, and procedures. In current years, IoT-based intelligent system is growing more dominant and significant due to machine learning. To recognize or predict the plant stress, many machine learning-based methodologies are introduced in every phase of an intelligent system for processing or analyzing the image or sensor-based data. Plant stress detection and recognition or predictions in time are based on the near field images or data. It is a very challenging task to segregate usable objects or data from its background. It is conventionally analyzed or measured by the naked eye or agricultural instruments and historical documents. In reality, these plant stress images or sensing data have a complex background. Without using IoT-based intelligent system, pre-processing and segmentation for complex backgrounds is time-consuming and has unsatisfactory achievability. Sometimes it is very difficult to focus on the effected portion in an image by reducing the background. Therefore, the upright methodologies are not very suitable for the plant stress management under the unvarying atmospheres. Motivated by the mechanism of stress identification based on IoT using machine learning, this study applied a review for stress detection and quantification to reach satisfactory results.

1.5 CONCLUSION

The internet is responsible for connecting our social and digital life, and this chapter includes a study over IoT-based intelligent system for agriculture. It is maintained through different digital devices connected through the internet and has a great scope to positively impact on the agricultural process, which actually brings benefits to the social life. IoT-based intelligent system is helpful for the detection of plant stress and the sharing of that information with the farmer. If implemented in real life, then it may be very useful to reduce the human effort in the field. The automation in the agricultural field may be possible through the use of this model. Especially when it comes to detecting the plant stress, this model is very helpful. It also shares its detailed analysis with the farmer, which makes farmer's jobs easier. In the future scope over this model, the implementation of the robotic system is also feasible, which ultimately reduces the human effort. Most interestingly, the implementation of all these advanced technologies also take care of the environment. The quality production can be achieved with this IoT-based intelligent system, and hence the method is justified for implementing in the real world. The future work of this should be directed towards the statistical analysis of different machine learning models for plant stress detection and how it is affecting the production in a cost-effective way.

REFERENCES

1. Tzounis, A., Katsoulas, N., Bartzanas, T., and Kittas, C. 2017. Internet of Things in agriculture, recent advances and future challenges. *Biosystems Engineering.* 164 (December): 31–48.
2. Steensland, A., and Zeigler, M. 2017. *A World of Productive Sustainable Agriculture.* 2017 GAP Report. Global Harvest Initiative, Washington, DC. 1–69. https://www.globalharvestinitiative.org/gap-report-gap-index/2017-gap-report/ (accessed May 12, 2019).
3. Behmann, J., Mahlein, A., Rumpf, T., Römer, C., and Plümer, L. 2015. A review of advanced machine learning methods for the detection of biotic stress in precision crop protection. *Precision Agriculture.* 16: 239–260.

4. Lee, M., and Yoe, H. 2015. Analysis of environmental stress factors using an artificial growth system and plant fitness optimization. *BioMed Research International.* doi: 10.1155/2015/292543 (accessed May 18, 2019).
5. Govender, M., Dye, P.J., Weiersbye, I.M., Witkowski, E.T.F., and Ahmed, F. 2009. Review of commonly used remote sensing and ground-based technologies to measure plant water stress. *Water SA.* 35(5): 741–752.
6. Pinter, P.J., Stanghellini, M.E., Reginato, R.J., Idso, S.B., Jenkins, A.D., and Jackson, R.D. 1979. Remote detection of biological stresses in plants with infrared thermometry. *Science.* 205(4406): 585–587.
7. Guo, P., Dusadeeringsikul, P.O., and Nof, S.Y. 2018. Agricultural cyber physical system collaboration for greenhouse stress management. *Computers and Electronics in Agriculture.* 150: 439–454.
8. Lee, W.S., Alchanatis, V., Yang, C., Hirafuji, M., Moshou, D., and Li, C. 2010. Sensing technologies for precision specialty crop production. *Computers and Electronics in Agriculture.* 74: 2–33.
9. Leinonen, I., and Jones, H.G. 2004. Combining thermal and visible imagery for estimating canopy temperature and identifying plant stress. *Journal Experimental Botany.* 55: 1423–1431.
10. Casanova, J.J. et al. 2014. Development of a wireless computer vision instrument to detect biotic stress in wheat. *Sensors (Basel).* 2014: 17753–17769.
11. Belforte, G., Gay, P., and Aimonino, D.R. 2006. Robotics for improving quality, safety and productivity in intensive agriculture: Challenges and opportunities. In *Industrial Robotics: Programming, Simulation and Applications, Advanced Robotic Systems.* Kin, Huat Low (Ed.). Vienna, Austria. https://www.intechopen.com/books/industrial_robotics_programming_simulation_and_applications/robotics_for_improving_quality__safety_and_productivity_in_intensive_agriculture__challenges_and_opp (accessed May 20, 2019).
12. Behmann, J. et al. 2014. Ordinal classification for efficient plant stress prediction in hyperspectral data. *The International Archives of the Photogrammetry, Remote Sensing and Spatial Information Sciences.* XL-7: 29–36.
13. Hu, X., and Qian, S. 2011. IOT application system with crop growth models in facility agriculture. In *Proceedings of 6th International Conference on Computer Sciences and Convergence Information Technology, ICCIT.* 129–133.
14. Baranwal, T., and Pushpendra, K.P. 2016. Development of IoT based smart security and monitoring devices for agriculture. In *Cloud System and Big Data Engineering (Confluence), 2016 6th International Conference.* IEEE. 597–602. doi: 10.13140/RG.2.1.1449.8966 (accessed May 25, 2019).

15. De, S., Elsaleh, T., Barnaghi, P., and Meissner, S. 2012. An internet of things platform for real-world and digital objects. *Scalable Computing: Practice and Experience.* 13(1): 45–57.
16. Ray, P.P. 2018. A survey on Internet of Things architectures. *Journal of King Saud University – Computer and Information Sciences.* 30: 291–319.
17. Enji, S., Zhanga, X., and Lib, Z. 2012. The internet of things (IOT) and cloud computing (CC) based tailings dam monitoring and pre-alarm system in mines. *Safety Science.* 50(4): 811–815.
18. He, W., Yan, G., and Xu, L.D. 2014. Developing vehicular data cloud services in the IoT environment. *IEEE Transactions on Industrial Information.* 10(2): 1587–1595.
19. Atzori, L., Iera, A., and Morabito, G. 2010. The internet of things: A survey. *Computer Networks.* 54(15): 2787–2805.
20. Cai, K., Liang, X., and Wang, K. 2011. Development of field information monitoring system based on the internet of things. In *Intelligent Computing and Information Science (Part I).* Springer, Chongqing, China, 675–680.
21. Ma, J., Zhou, X., Li, S., and Li, Z. 2011. Connecting agriculture to the internet of things through sensor networks. In *Proceedings 2011 IEEE International Conferences on Internet of Things and Cyber, Physical and Social Computing,* Chen, R. (Ed.). iThings/CPSCom 2011. 184–187. doi: 10.1109/iThings/CPSCom.2011.32 (accessed May 22, 2019).
22. Fei, L., Vogler, M., Claessens, M., and Dustdar, S. 2013. Towards automated IoT application deployment by a cloud-based approach. In *Proceedings of IEEE 6th International Service-Oriented Computing and Applications (SOCA),* 61–68.
23. Bandyopadhyay, D., and Sen, J. 2011. Internet of things: Applications and challenges in technology and standardization. *Wireless Personal Communication.* 58(1): 49–69.
24. Holler, J. et al. 2014. *From Machine-to-Machine to the Internet of Things: Introduction to a New Age of Intelligence.* Elsevier, Atlanta.
25. Ma, C. et al. 2014. Machine learning for big data analytics in plants. *Trends Plant Science.* 19: 798–808.
26. Bannister, K., Giorgetti, G., and Gupta, S.K. 2008. Wireless sensor networking for hot applications: Effects of temperature on signal strength, data collection and localization. In *Proceedings of the 5th Workshop on Embedded Networked Sensors (HotEmNets 2008),* 1–5.
27. Andrews, M., Raven, J.A., and Lea, P.J. 2013. Do plants need nitrate? The mechanisms by which nitrogen form affects plants. *Annals of Applied Biology.* 163: 174–199.

28. Ali, I., Greifeneder, F., Stamenkovic, J., Neumann, M., and Notarnicola, C. 2015. Review of machine learning approaches for biomass and soil moisture retrievals from remote sensing data. *Remote Sensor.* 7(12): 16398–16421.

29. Hoshi, T., Ochi, S., Masuyama, T., Yasuba, K.I., Kurosaki, H., and Okayasu, T. 2016. Weatherability evaluation of low-cost relative humidity sensors for use in greenhouse environments. *Agriculture Information Research.* 25(3): 79–85.

30. Kozai, T., and Fujiwara, K. 2016. Moving toward self-learning closed plant production systems. In *LED Lighting for Urban Agriculture*, Kozai, T, Fujiwara, and K, Runkle, E.S. (Eds). Springer, Singapore, 445–448.

31. Jhuria, M., Kumar, A., and Borse, R. 2013. Image processing for smart farming: Detection of disease and fruit grading. In *2013 IEEE Second International Conference on Image Information Processing*, 521–526.

32. Nari, K., and Yang-Won, L. 2016. Machine learning approaches to corn yield estimation using satellite images and climate data: A case of IOWA state. *Journal of the Korean Society of Surveying Geodesy Photogrammetry and Cartography.* 34: 383–390.

33. Cai, J. et al. 2015. RootGraph: A graphic optimization tool for automated image analysis of plant roots. *Journal of Experimental Botany.* Published online July 29, 2015. doi: 10.1093/jxb/erv359 (accessed May 21, 2019).

34. Kruse, O.M.O. et al. 2014. Pixel classification methods for identifying and quantifying leaf surface injury from digital images. *Computers and Electronics in Agriculture.* 108: 155–165.

35. Bock, C. et al. 2010. Plant disease severity estimated visually, by digital photography and image analysis, and by hyperspectral imaging. *Critical Reviews in Plant Sciences.* 29: 59–107.

36. Scholes, J.D. 1992. Photosynthesis: Cellular and tissue aspects in diseased leaves. In *Pests and Pathogens: Plant Responses to Foliar Attack*, Ayres, P.G. (Ed.). Bios Scientific Publishers, Oxford, 85–106.

37. Baranowski, P. et al. 2015. Hyper spectral and thermal imaging of oilseed rape (Brassica napus) response to fungal species of the genus Alternaria. *PLoS ONE.* 10(3): 1–19.

38. Kouche, A.E. 2012. Towards a wireless sensor network platform for the Internet of things: Sprouts WSN platform. In *Proceedings of IEEE international conference on communications (ICC)*, 632–636.

39. Yaacoub, E., Kadri, A., and Dayya, A.D. 2012. Cooperative wireless sensor networks for green internet of things. In *Proceedings of the 8th ACM Symposium on QoS and Security for Wireless and Mobile Networks*, 79–80.

40. Ruiz-Garcia, L., Lunadei, L., Barreiro, P., and Robla, J.I. 2009. Review of wireless sensor technologies and applications in agriculture and food industry: State of the art and current trends. *Sensors*. 9: 4728–4750.
41. Li, L. et al. 2014. A review of imaging techniques for plant phenotyping. *Sensors*. 2014: 20078–20111.
42. Camargo, A. and Smith, J.S. 2009. An image processing based algorithm to automatically identify plant disease visual symptoms. *Biosystems Engineering*. 102: 9–21.
43. Römer, C. et al. 2012. Early drought stress detection in cereals: Simplex volume maximisation for hyper spectral image analysis. *Functional Plant Biology*. 39: 878–890.
44. González-Pérez, J.L. et al. 2013. Color image segmentation using perceptual spaces through applets for determining and preventing diseases in chili peppers. *The African Journal of Biotechnology*. 12: 679–688.
45. Zhang, J., Li, A., Li, J., Yang, Q., and Gang, C. 2011. Research of real-time image acquisition system based on ARM 7 for agricultural environmental monitoring. In *2011 International Conference on Remote Sensing, Environment and Transportation Engineering (RSETE)*, 6216–6220. doi: 10.1109/RSETE.2011.5965777 (accessed May 22, 2019).
46. Popovic, T., Latinovic, N., Pešic, A., Zecevic, Z., Krstajic, B., and Djukanovic, S. 2017. Architecting an IoT-enabled platform for precision agriculture and ecological monitoring: A case study. *Computers and Electronics in Agriculture*. 140: 255–265.
47. Singh, A., Ganapathy Subramanian, B., Singh, A.K., and Sarkar, S. 2019. Machine learning for high-throughput stress phenotyping in plants. *Trends in Plant Science*, TRPLSC 1361. doi: 10.1016/j.tplants.2015.10.015 (accessed May 21, 2019).
48. Chlingaryan, A., Sukkarieh, S., and Whelan, B. 2018. Machine-learning approaches for crop yield prediction and nitrogen status estimation in precision agriculture: A review. *Computers and Electronics in Agriculture*. 151: 61–69.
49. Miorandi, D., Sicari, S., and Chlamtac, I. 2012. Internet of things: Vision, applications and research challenges. *Ad Hoc Network*. 10(7): 1497–1516.
50. Rao, B.P., Saluia, P., Sharma, N., Mittal, A., and Sharma, S.V. 2012. Cloud computing for internet of things sensing based applications. In *Proceedings of 2012 Sixth International Conference on Sensing Technology (ICST)*, 374–380.
51. Shang, X., Zhang, R., and Chen, Y. 2012. Internet of things (IoT) service architecture and its application in E-Commerce. *Journal of Electronic Commerce in Organizations (JECO)*. 10(3): 44–55.

52. Zhao, J.C., Zhang, J.F., Feng, Y., and Guo, J.X. 2010. The study and application of the IOT technology in agriculture. In *Proceedings of 3rd IEEE International Conference on Computer Science and Information, Technology (ICCSIT)*, vol. 2, 462–465.
53. Emmi, L. et al. 2014. Configuring a fleet of ground robots for agricultural tasks. In *Advances in Intelligent Systems and Computing. robot2013: First Iberian Robotics Conference*, Armada, M.A. et al. (Eds.). Springer, 505–517.
54. Kaundal, R. et al. 2006. Machine learning techniques in disease forecasting: A case study on rice blast prediction. *BMC Bioinformatics*. 7: 1–16.
55. Holmgren, P., and Thuresson, T. 1998. Satellite remote sensing for forestry planning—A review. *Scandinavian Journal of Forest Research*. 13: 90–110.
56. Seelan, S.K., Laguette, S., Casady, G.M., and Seielstad, G.A. 2003. Remote sensing applications for precision agriculture: A learning community approach. *Remote Sensor Environment*. 88: 157–169.
57. Mohanty, S.P., Hughes, D.P., and Salathé, M. 2016. Using deep learning for image-based plant disease detection. *Frontiers Plant Science*. 7. doi: 10.3389/fpls.2016.01419 (accessed May 19, 2019).
58. Jhuria, M., Kumar, A., and Borse, R. 2013. Image processing for smart farming: Detection of disease and fruit grading. In *2013 IEEE Second International Conference on Image Information Processing*, 521–526.
59. Montalvo, M. et al. 2013. Automatic expert system for weeds/crops identification in images from maize fields. *Expert Systems With Applications*. 40(1): 75–82.
60. Nari, K., and Yang-Won, L. 2016. Machine learning approaches to corn yield estimation using satellite images and climate data: A case of Iowa state. *Journal of the Korean Society of Surveying Geodesy Photogrammetry and Cartography*. 34: 383–390.
61. Mohanty, S.P., Hughes, D.P., and Salathé, M. 2016. Using deep learning for image-based plant disease detection. *Frontiers Plant Science*. 7. doi: 10.3389/fpls.2016.01419 (accessed May 19, 2019).
62. Leinonen, I., and Jones, H.G. 2005. Combining thermal and visible imagery for estimating canopy temperature and identifying plant stress. *Journal of Experimental Botany*. 55(401): 1423–1431.
63. Omasa, K. 1990. Image instrumentation methods of plant analysis. In *Modern Methods of Plant Analysis*, Liskens, H.F., Jackson, J.F. (Eds.). Springer-Verlag, Berlin, 203–243.
64. Bock, C. et al. 2010. Plant disease severity estimated visually, digital photography and image analysis, and by hyper spectral imaging. *Critical Reviews in Plant Sciences*. 29: 59–107.

65. González-Pérez, J.L. et al. 2013. Color image segmentation using perceptual spaces through applets for determining and preventing diseases in chili peppers. *African Journal of Biotechnology*. 12: 679–688.
66. Tian, L.F., and Slaughter, D.C. 1998. Environmentally adaptive segmentation algorithm for outdoor image segmentation. *Computers and Electronics in Agriculture*. 21: 153–168.
67. Onyango, C.M., and Marchant, J.A. 2003. Segmentation of row crop plants from weeds using color and morphology. *Computers and Electronics in Agriculture*. 39: 141–155.
68. Bulanon, D.M., Kataoka, T., Ota, Y., and Hiroma, T. 2002. Segmentation algorithm for the automatic recognition of Fuji apples at harvest. *Biosystems Engineering*. 83: 405–412.
69. Huang, K.-Y. 2007. Application of artificial neural network for detecting Phalaenopsis seedling diseases using color and texture features. *Computers and Electronics in Agriculture*. 57: 3–11.
70. Larios, N. et al. 2010. Haar random forest features and SVM spatial matching kernel for stonefly species identification. In *Proceedings of the 2010 20th International Conference on Pattern Recognition*. IEEE Computer Society, 2624–2627.
71. Muhammed, H.H., and Larsolle, A. 2003. Feature vector based analysis of hyper spectral crop reflectance data for discrimination and quantification of fungal disease severity in wheat. *Biosystems Engineering*. 86(2): 125–134.
72. Ruß, G., and Kruse, R. 2010. Feature selection for wheat yield prediction. In *Research and Development in Intelligent Systems XXVI: Incorporating Applications and Innovations in Intelligent Systems XVII*. Bramer, M., Ellis, R., Petridis, M. (Eds.). Springer, London, 465–478.
73. Fu, B. 2012. Research on the agriculture intelligent system based on IOT. In *Proceedings of 2012 International Conference on Image Analysis and Signal Processing, IASP 2012*. 386–389.
74. Shekoofa, A. et al. 2014. Determining the most important physiological and agronomic traits contributing to maize grain yield through machine learning algorithms: A new avenue in intelligent agriculture. *PLoS ONE*. 9(5): 1–9. doi: 10.1371/journal. pone.0097288 (accessed May 19, 2019).
75. Gonzalez-Sanchez, A. et al. 2014. Predictive ability of machine learning methods for massive crop yield prediction. *Spanish Journal of Agricultural Research*. 12: 313–328.
76. Goldstein, A., Fink, L., Meitin, A., Bohadana, S., Lutenberg, O., and Ravid, G. 2017. Applying machine learning on sensor data for irrigation recommendations: Revealing the agronomist's tacit knowledge. *Precision Agriculture*. 19(3): 421–444.

77. Mehra, L.K., Cowger, C., Gross, K., and Ojiambo, P.S. 2016. Predicting pre-planting risk of stagonospora nodorum blotch in winter wheat using machine-learning models. *Frontiers in Plant Science.* 7: 1–14.
78. Morellos, A., Pantazi, X.E., Moshou, D., Alexandridis, T., Whetton, R., Tziotzios, G., Wiebensohn, J., Bill, R., and Mouazen, A.M. 2016. Machine learning based prediction of soil total nitrogen, organic carbon and moisture content by using VIS-NIR spectroscopy. *Biosystems Engineering.* 152: 104–116.
79. Peña, J., Gutiérrez, P., Hervás-Martínez, C., Six, J., Plant, R., and López-Granados, F. 2014. Object-based image classification of summer crops with machine learning methods. *Remote Sensor.* 6(6): 5019–5041.
80. Subhadra, M., Debahuti, M., and Gour Hari, S. 2016. Applications of machine learning techniques in agricultural crop production: A review paper. *Indian Journal of Science and Technology.* 9(38): 1–14.

2

IoT: A STEP TOWARDS SUSTAINABILITY

Vikram Kulkarni and Rejo Mathew

CONTENTS

2.1 INTRODUCTION

According to the UN Vision 2030, the SDGs were defined to make the planet prosper with harmony, peace, and lessened carbon emissions. The UN has defined 17 major goals for SDGs, as shown in Figure 2.1 [1]. The Internet of Things (IoT) is considered as the most significant component that shall coordinate the SDGs. The World Economic Forum (WEF) has assessed the impact of IoT-relative

United Nations – Sustainability Development Goals Vision - 2030		
1. Clean Water and Sanitation	2. Affordable and Clean Power	3. Industry innovation and Infrastructure
4. Sustainable Cities and Communities	5. Climate Action	6. Life below water
7. Life on Land	8. Responsible Consumption and Production	9. Good Health
10. Reduced inequalities	11. No Poverty	12. Zero Hunger
13. Quality Education	14. Gender Equality	15. Decent work and Economic Growth
16. Peace, Justice and Strong in Situations	17. Partnership Goals	

Figure 2.1 United Nations Commission Sustainable Development Goals.

innovations on UN-SDGs [2]. The evaluation of WEF is based on the assessment shown in Figure 2.2. In these modern days, the population prefer to live in cities; hence, this is becoming a major challenge to maintain the natural resources (clean air and water), infrastructure management, etc. [3].

2.2 IoT FOR REDUCING POVERTY OR NO POVERTY

As per the World Inequality Report 2018, despite improved technology and standards of living the inequality between the rich and poor is widening daily in all world regions at different speeds [4]. As per the United Nations Populations Fund (UNFPA), in the Least Developed Countries (LDCs), the economy is growing at a snail's pace, whereas the population is doubling each year. The rising population is compounding problems, leading to acute shortage of basic facilities and depriving people access to already depleted resources [5].

Poverty includes lack of water and lack of food, leading to malnutrition, as well as lack of basic necessities that a human being deserves. Conflicts, regional tensions, and wars add to the woes. South Asia and Sub-Saharan Africa are the most affected areas and consist of the highest number of people below the poverty line. Lack of financial inclusion, access to government services, and access to clean energy keeps the poor away from the government. Total income of nearly one percent of the richest countries in the world is needed to eradicate poverty, i.e., about US$175 billion to end extreme poverty in 20 years. The statistics from South Africa throw some light. Out of 66% of the population below 35 years of age, 50% are unemployed. Digital

Figure 2.2 World Economic Forum assessment on the impact of IoT-relative innovations on UN-SDGs.

revolution is the new driver for economic growth. Internet is neither affordable nor accessible in the Least Developed Countries. The most expensive internet rates are in Sub-Saharan Africa, which is also one reason why less than 10% of its population has internet access [6]. Despite all that, IoT is contributing immensely by empowering areas like education and healthcare, advancing disaster readiness, strengthening economies, expanding green cover, and facilitating inclusive growth and greater accountability. Online and geospatial data collection and analysis gives an impetus for effective policymaking. It alleviates the impact of natural disasters, responds to epidemics, and improves standards of education. At the Mobile World Congress held in Barcelona in 2018, the World Bank Group and the Global System for Mobile Communications Association (GSMA) decided to partner and begin new initiatives in field of IoT [7].

2.2.1 Financial Inclusion

Access to bank accounts and mobile services helps the government to reach out to the deprived. The United Nations Global Pulse and National Statistics mines mobile phone data to check household data consumption and monitor socioeconomic behavior across world [8].

Biometric identification systems guarantee that money reaches the right hands; as a result, enabling them to decide and control their expenses, e.g., Aadhaar (World's Largest Biometric ID Program) in India [9] and National Database and Registration Authority (NADRA) in Pakistan [10].

Direct money transfer and basic financial services avoids delay and curbs corruption. M-pesa in Kenya [11], AlibabasAlipay in China [12], Easypaisa in Pakistan [13], and DBTBharat [14] from the Indian government give the needy access to more than 500 schemes. Village Pay phone program in Bangladesh [15] is another example.

2.2.2 Access to Government Services

Geo-tagged information from mobiles delivers location-specific data about environmental challenges, government services, water resources, etc. The overall figures indicate what works and aids people to see results and hold administration accountable. For example, Nigeria's SMDG Information Base, started in 2015. Government schemes, awareness on social issues and public concerns are put across using talk shows and interactive programs on community radio stations. For example, in Uganda, people often raise apprehensions and express their views. The United Nations Global Pulse uses voice recognition software to study inclinations, comprehend gender biases, and eventually update policy measures to alleviate poverty [16]. In India, the Prime Minister addresses the nation and emphasizes on improving living standards by publicizing government schemes [17]. In Kenya the government displays information on its ICT website [18].

The 2013 Telecommunications Law passed by government of Myanmar improved the number of mobile subscribers from 1.2% in 2013 to 15% in 2015. The Government issued a directive that 10 million new users should be women, and also established funds as backup to rural areas [19].

2.2.3 Clean Environment and Clean Energy

• Pollution from cook stoves that burn fuel from biomass such as wood or animal dung kills 4.3 million people globally per year—more than malaria, TB, and HIV/AIDS combined.
• In India, IoT devices were provided to identify homes with toxic levels of air pollution, then intervened with cash incentives to encourage people to shift to clean cooking and heating.
• IoT is playing a big role in renewable energy resources [20, 21].

2.2.4 Rescue Operations

In the Least Developed Countries, the UN collaborates with private mobile companies to pay people working in disaster relief areas where access would be difficult and terrains difficult to cover. During Typhoon Haiyan in the Philippines, Google Person Finder as well as Digital Humanitarian Network (DHN) was pressed into action [22]. Saving lives with massive IoT, in China, movement of land is monitored by IoT narrowband sensors which collect data and trigger the alarm to areas; this helps during massive landslides and earthquakes saving lives [23, 24].

2.3 ZERO HUNGER

The way to end hunger is by attaining food safety and enriched nutrition, as well as stimulating viable agriculture. Zero Hunger Goal (ZHG) was propelled by UN Secretary-General Ban Ki-moon in 2012. The ZHG focusses on maintainable and weather-compatible agriculture traditions, including through spreading production, growing smallholders' income and productivity, growing decent rural employment, minimizing food losses, improving access to adequate food and healthy diets, for all, and an end to underfeeding in all its forms.

Geographic information system (GIS) and satellite images of land, along with environment information, is collected and mapped, and target areas are identified for agriculture. This information is used by governments for decision-making. Greenhouse automation and IoT-based products like Farmapp [25], Growlink [26], GreenIQ [27] use sensors to collect data and help to manage water and lighting conditions on farms.

IFAD and Intel have partnered to provide software to farmers in Cambodia to examine earth, decide fertilizer requirements, offer guidance on finest seeds, and tackle pests and diseases—Arable [28] and Semios [29] are products which forecast and act as benchmarks. People are trained to access and market their products. The software guides farmers on what is best suited for their farm; it also provides information about local suppliers. It helps farmers cut down their costs and avoid overuse of fertilizers. In India there is also Android app-based software that has helped farmers to improve the production by 300%. Governments are investing heavily in prediction problem tree exploration and climate change susceptibility planning; IoT-based agro products like *allMeteo* [30], *Smart Elements* [31], and *Pycno* [32] are being widely used for linking satellite imaging, GIS modelling, and social vulnerability surveys. They help categorize communities and target areas based on their exposure to climate change, and plan to erect retaining walls, dry wall terraces, water catchment ponds, and other important arrangements based on the needs of the rural population. It cuts preconceptions in designing projects and sets an outstanding landmark in the promotion of observing and assessment systems to estimate project accomplishments. GIS demonstrating approaches can and are being extended to other vulnerabilities.

Farm animals are indispensable to every farmer. Monitoring their health and managing them is critical to growth. Smart agriculture sensors (collar tags) like *SCR* [33], *Cowlar* [34], and *Vet Africa* [35] monitor health, activity, and nutrition insights on farm animals. Mobile apps provide timely animal disease broadcasting to boost surveillance and quick cautioning of epidemics in animals, comprising zoonotic diseases causing a potential public health threat, and facilitates governments to warn vulnerable residents. Event Mobile Application (EMA-i) developed by the Food Administration of the United Nations is used widely across the globe [36]. Farm productivity management systems like *FarmLogs* [37], *Cropio* [38], *Agrivi* [39], and *Conservis* [40] use a number of agriculture IoT devices and sensors powered by analytical features and accurate reporting facilities to monitor remote farms and streamline all farm activities. In Japan, the government has pushed tech giants for IoT farming. Fujitsu's Akisai software exposes farmers to smart agriculture [41]. New age farming has been initiated in the Middle East by Sharp Electronics [42]. Vertical farming has been done by Panasonic in Singapore warehouses [43]. Toshiba's factory farm has been creating news across the world [44].

Ericsson's IoT Accelerator platform enabled with artificial intelligence (AI) integrates new IoT devices, optimizes agricultural processes, and provides instant access to devices after installation [45]. The information system agencies like GIEWS [46], DLIS [47], CCIAA have added new dimensions to farm operations and sustainable living. *Agricultural Market Information System (AMIS)* [48] ensures transparency in food markets. It helps all agro-based economies to monitor and trade supplies, especially rice, wheat, maize and pulses. It helps in policymaking during crises, strengthening global food security, and mitigates price rises. *E-Agriculture Strategy Guide* [49], used for Asia Pacific countries, focusses on ICT in agriculture and modernizing agriculture and giving livelihood to rural populations. Farmers are provided with information across all the developing economies via the internet, email, SMS and mobile phones about the key people in the marketplace chain, as well as processors, agents, and consumers. Their feedback clearly shows there is a substantial effect on their production, incomes, and entry into markets. *I-cow* [50], Cameroon's *M-Farm* [51], *Esoko* [52], *AgroHub* [53], World Cocoa Foundation App for Ghana [54], *Kilimo Salama* [55], *Kuza Doctor* [56] text-based agriculture education platform, and Botswana startup *Modisar* [57] are already pioneering the cause of IoT-based farming.

2.4 GOOD HEALTH AND WELL-BEING

IoT has revolutionized the healthcare sector by reducing time and costs, improving treatments, optimizing workflows, obtaining accuracy in reporting, and facilitating ease in disease monitoring and surveillance. IoT-based healthcare promotion is forecasted to be US$600 billion by 2025, expanding at a compound annual growth rate (CAGR) of 20.2%. Clinical operations, inpatient monitoring, medication management, connected imaging, and telemedicine are major areas of IoT applications [58]. The IoT healthcare market is growing remarkably at a CAGR of 37% [59]. Biosensors, smart and wearable devices, web portals, mobile apps, virtual home assistants, blockchain-based health record systems and predictive analysis aids to spread awareness and get medical facilities.

Wearable sensors and smart devices give accurate readings, and interpretation of their results is done using mobile devices which enable medical centers to substitute bulky medical gear with smaller devices. Elderly patients suffering from critical ailments must have such handy devices. Biosensors collect data of sleep timings, all activities, and overall health. Users can check blood pressure, heart-beat, alcohol level in blood, glucose levels, oxygen level, pulse, and alert others (and doctors) if any anomaly is detected. Smart devices in healthcare devices like smart inhalers were introduced for decreasing the effects of bronchial asthma. The diabetes-based problems are addressed by modern syringe pens. The smart blister and smart pills were also introduced in the market to address the issues of health.

Frontline health workers use IoT-enabled devices to identify and diagnose pneumonia and preeclampsia. Preeclampsia is spreading widely and is becoming a cause for maternal deaths. Online health portals allow patients to get lab results, schedule appointments, and consult with experts, who can provide tips and food recipes for a healthy life. When the IoT is working for the accumulation of data, the integration of blockchain concepts will make it more efficient. Estonian eHealth Foundation and Guardtime company have created a blockchain-based system to safeguard millions of medical records [60]. During epidemics, mobile data helps predict, prepare, and prevent the spreading of deadly diseases, track movement of people and limit the areas affected and provide medicines and take preventive measures like vaccination based on intelligent data analytics. Some popular examples lately are Ebola in West Africa [61], Zika virus [62], and H1N1 or swine flu [63], which affected so many lives across globe. Supply chain companies like Controlant have a web-enabled cloud platform with intelligent analytics, and use wireless and reusable data loggers that measure environmental conditions and product movement, along with 24/7 customer support [64].

Nokia are working on IoT to curb disease outbreak [65]. Digital payment to those involved in prevention and critical services, especially during Ebola, facilitated them to come across their own requirements and afford continuous care. Ericsson donated more than 1,300 mobile phones that were pre-loaded by employee volunteers with apps on Ebola prevention and treatment as well as a survey tool from the Earth Institute and the International Rescue Committee (IRC). The phones were shipped to UNICEF and IRC for deployment to community health workers in West Africa. Nearly 1,300 community health workers benefitted from smartphones configured by Ericsson volunteers [66].

MedRec Project is a decentralized patient medical record distribution system with a high-security level system for healthcare data access [67]. IoT plays a major role for vaccination by monitoring the supply chain [68, 69]. Initiatives like iHub Kenya deploys young entrepreneurs to invent ICT solutions that link marginalized groups to critical services like healthcare and education [70]. Schemes like RTHS [71, 72], EMS [73, 74] CHS [75], and eHealth helps in sector-wise planning. The coordination of distributed district health schemes are improving the ability to plan, budget, and deliver people-centric services. Telemedicine provides medical advice and treatment options access to all people across the globe.

Training for nurses and paramedical staff has been a concern which has been addressed by IoT, the best example being Guatemala, where more than 300 aspiring nurses were trained to handle patients via distance education using mobile devices. Qualified trained staff with ultramodern facilities are key to healthcare [76]. Online medical libraries and resources are available at low cost to health researchers and workers across the globe, contributing essential knowledge resources on health. Health Internetwork Access to Research Initiative (HINARI) [77], Human Health Campus (HHC) [78], Distance Assisted Training Online (DATOL) [79], A pilot e-learning program VUCCnet, initiated for training professionals for comprehensive cancer control [80], are few examples.

Mobile applications for medical experts are launched and used by experts across the globe. Cancer Staging Apps like TNM [81, 82] and FIGO [83, 84], as well as NUCARD [85, 86], an app for the management of cardiovascular diseases, are available on the App Store as well as the Play Store. Africa Radiation Oncology Network (AFRONET) is a telemedicine project for African radiotherapists highlighting the latest developments in medicine along with consultations across the globe [87]. Pharmaceutical companies are streamlining clinical trials and decision-making processes with the use of artificial intelligence and IoT. Human error has reduced as intelligent data analytics collect and segregate data from various sources and apply various algorithms to make data processing effective.

2.5 QUALITY EDUCATION

Education empowers individuals, augments health and productivity, and fortifies societies and economies. The aim of education is to strengthen current systems; augment knowledge dissemination; broaden access to information, improved quality, and efficient learning; and ensure more effective service provision. Governments must reform curricula and assessment and should make use of ICT apps and incentivize educators who employ latest pedagogies. Online learning, especially Massive Open Online Course (MOOCs), provide free access to top quality training materials and mentors accessible over the internet via wireless devices. It also allows students to enroll and break distance barriers and save valuable time [88]. The adoption of interoperability standards has changed academic structures and broken conventional ideas, particularly with the introduction Open Source Software (OSS) learning [89]. The *World's Largest Lesson* (WLL) is latest platform which reaches out to children across globe [90]. Train the Teacher programs empowers teachers and helps them upgrade their skills and thereby impart quality education to their students. There are several such programs conducted across the world. The UNESCO initiated ICT-CFT for promoting the competency-based approach for the effective pedagogical use of ICTs. Mobiles offer an almost free means for providing in-service support to teachers, particularly in the case of the low-income countries [91].

UNESCO has successfully initiated and driven teacher development programs through mobile phone–based learning. UNESCO has initiated this process particularly in low-income countries like Mexico [92], Nigeria [93], Pakistan [94], West African States (ECOWAS), and Guinea [95]. In parts of Africa, a UNESCO China Funds-in-Trust project with a funding of US$8 million is harnessing quality education using technology [96]. In Myanmar, UNESCO, with the project supported with Australian funds, is working with the Ministry of Education to influence growth in access to ICTs from beginning to end, strengthening pre-service teacher training [97]. *Jaago Foundation*, Bangladesh, is a brilliant example of reaching out to the underprivileged children in rural areas. It provides a high-quality study program free-of-cost taught by quality teachers in urban areas via videoconferencing [98].

In Jordan, an open source education management information system has improved the quality of education; it is based on the Internet of Teaching Services [99]. Kiron Open Higher Education for refugees in Germany is designed for educating refugees. Qualifying refugees pick courses corresponding to their conditions and requirements, and are encouraged by a coaching service to take on online learning [100]. *"Can't wait to learn"* initiatives spread across 20 countries use solar-powered tablets with self-paced software that is easy to operate and is very interactive; this helped Sudanese primary school prospectus. The children are trained to use digital tablets in community spaces by trained facilitator-based apps—this has increased the value of digital devices [101]. *U-Report*, a social messaging tool, allows young people to record their opinions and offer essential perception data about troubles in their society [102]. *EduTrac* initiative in Peru uses SMS-based technology to gather data in remote communities, tracks attendance, and ensures timely delivery of school materials. It is a comprehensive way to advance school quality in areas far from urban cities [103]. Ericsson has opened eHub in South Africa; it consists of digital resources, training, and mentorship for up-and-coming entrepreneurs [104]. Connect to Learn is an ICT learning cloud solution from Ericsson which empowers teachers and gives students access to global resources [105].

2.6 GENDER EQUALITY

When the woman of a nation grow, the nation prospers as well. The major lacuna are low literacy levels, economic-strength, and undelivered assurance to gender fairness in policy decisions. The gender gap for access to internet is *11.6%* globally and *32.9%* in LDCs (ITU, 2017). Adequate budget allocation and timely gender-based data collection is essential to bridge the gender gap. Traditional methods like admin data and surveys among woman are still used for policymaking. But with rapid use of technology, social media data, medical records, TV and radio interaction data, mobile phone usage data, and mobile phone surveys, are big data sources and are analyzed to design inclusive and timely woman-empowering policies [106]. IoT tender vast prospective for women: improving education and health, decreasing poverty, increasing agricultural yield, and creating respectable jobs. The *Virtual Skills School "We Learn"* initiative offers another opportunity to women who left formal education. It facilitates their association into formal schooling and learning processes. It also allows them to understand non-traditional sectors and progress them to improve their economic condition. Digital and financial literacy are the major focus areas [107]. *HeForShe IMPACT 10x10x10* works with high-talented communities that ensure game-changing gender equality commitments [108]. The *EmpowerWoman #HerStory* movement showcases the success stories of influential women to motivate and connect women from various domains and geographical areas. This data is analyzed to identify gender disparity in health, learning, and industry markets [109]. Women are largely employed in the informal sector in most countries. Women's organizations like *SEWA* and *WIEGO* have completely digitized the entire sector, thus creating more jobs and more entrepreneurs [110, 111]. *Million Kitchen*, based in India, is a social enterprise food-ordering platform that enables home-cooked meals prepared by low-income women to be delivered at home or at work [112]. *Home Foodies*, based out of Pakistan, is a pioneering food-ordering platform which links home-based women in the informal food industry to a wider pool of customers, and provides a safe virtual marketplace for them to sell their meals [113]. *GirlsGoIT* is an IoT-based project from the Republic of Moldova that is encouraging the girls to use digital and IT skills. Also, it is promoting entrepreneurial skills and particularly upholds optimistic models through the internet and online videos [114]. In Kenya and South Africa, about 20 Mozilla Clubs teach simple coding and digital knowledge skills for women and girls [115]. Rwandan women are trained in digital technologies and their efficient usage. This training program is sponsored by world organizations like WFP, FAO, and IFAD. With the knowledge from digital technology, about 70 percent of women are benefitting and are actively participating in development programs of nation also. Today, about 3,500 women are connected through mobile technology; also, these women have a great impact on the Rwanda farmers, and presently they support about 20 farmer cooperatives [116]. A computer and mobile-based literacy program was initiated for women by the Ministry of Education in Senegal. Due to huge success, this idea was also adopted by Nigeria, encouraging 60,000 girls and women in the context for improving their knowledge using digital knowledge [117]. To encourage woman in STEM, there is a Centre of Excellence set up by the United States in Texas, encouraging them to work on coding, botany, chemistry, and more [118]. *Connect to Learn* (a public-private collaboration by The Earth Institute at Columbia University, Ericsson, and Millennium Promise) provides financial support and scholarships to girls across Ghana, Tanzania, and Myanmar to complete their secondary education. Through these scholarships, girls can further their education and improve skills and employability [119].

Gender inequality is still a major problem in many countries. Modern technology in its many forms, like ICT, is trying to reform and redefine the way we are living and working. The connection between ICT and women's empowerment was undoubtedly reflected in the UN mission for Sustainability, Development and Growth as Goal 5. Gender equality is an important issue is to ensure that there is no one left behind. The authors in [120] have clearly explained the word empowerment means. Empowerment means development socially, economically, and psychologically. The internet is a powerful medium that connects each other.

J. E. Fountain (2000) [121] has presented an exclusive study on *"Constructing the Information Society: Women, Information Technology, and Design."* This study has focused importantly on the influence of women on the human capital requirements working society. The study has focused on how the presence and participation of women as experts, owners, and designers in the technology area are strengthening the field. Stronger representation by the female gender in important roles would help to restore a concerning human capital shortfall. It is anticipated that women are going to emerge as a large fragment on the internet in the next 20 years. The study identifies the accessibility of ICT to rural women, how it is showing impact on promoting gender equality, and also how it is ensuring the empowerment of women. Information technology has brought great changes in everyday life and has empowered women across the world. Close observation of the scenario in India indicates that states like Telangana, Andhra Pradesh, Tamil Nadu, Maharashtra, and Kerala are marching ahead in the field of ICT because of high female literacy levels.

Government of India initiatives for empowerment of women:

1. Government has a special concern for female education, particularly post-graduation (PG) and research.
2. Karnataka State Women's Development Corporation has initiated *e-mahile project* for women over 11 districts. Under this project, each woman registered in the society is given a free laptop, camera, printer, and projector for their professional use and growth
3. A UNESCO project called *"Networking Rural Women and Knowledge"* in Nabanna, India, is a great case. The purpose of this project is to build women's ICT-based information networks by providing facilities and training. The result of this is that the group of women earn more respect in their local societies [122].

Also, there are some apps that make the women feel more safe and confident. The best safety apps for women in India are *My Safetipin, Smart24x7, Himma, Raksha, bSafe, Nirbhaya: Be Fearless, Shake2Safety.*

2.7 IoT FOR CLEAN WATER AND SANITATION

Based on rough estimation figures from the non-profit organization The Water Project, one in nine of the world population does not have admittance to safe and purified drinking water. Figure 2.3 shows how rural people are using unfiltered water for drinking purposes.

2.7.1 Clean Water and Sanitation

A Gambia-based company has introduced the IoT-based *eWATER* system. Mobile technology is utilized for justifiable water conservation, and has identified that IoT can also influence and assure on clean water to all the countries that greatly need it. eWATER has emerged as one of the advanced water-supplying company based on IoT which supports money payments online, order online, etc. [123].

2.7.2 IoT Intelligence Is Revolutionizing the Water Industry

Based on the estimate from the IoT industry, by 2025 almost half of the population will opt to live in urban areas. Most of the urban areas are considered as water-stressed areas. Water resources are considered a very precious commodity and are becoming scarce rapidly. Thus, IoT-based smart water management solutions are becoming very important in order to the anticipated water crisis [124].

Figure 2.3 People consuming water from well in Africa.

Till now, the water industry was primarily dependent only on the Supervisory Control and Data Acquisition (SCADA) system which was unable to monitor the entire water distribution system due to the practical limitation of its installation points. Biz4Intellia, an end-to-end IoT solution, ensures improved smart water management through IoT water sensors which are installed at various locations in the IoT water system to sense any leakage or other malfunctions. *Biz4Intellia* already has pre-configured complete IoT Business Solution for water industry which can be implemented for various business cases in weeks instead of months. The IoT smart water management techniques can reduce water cost by up to 20 percent, resulting in better revenues with lower costs. IoT smart water management system also provides opportunities to municipalities to reduce operational costs around construction, maintenance, and more. *Biz4Intellia* out of the box solution integrates with more than 150 water sensors, including smart water meter, smart irrigation controller, IoT water flow meters, and IoT Water Valve [125].

Smart water distribution system can be formed with the help of data gathered from smart sensors. Distribution lines, embedded with pressure sensors, IoT water flow meter, and electrically actuated valves, control the flow of the water supply in real time. With smart water distribution system, customers have attained following business benefits by implementing *Biz4Intellia*'s smart water distribution management solution achieve:

- Reduced water wastage with features like predictive maintenance, remote controlling, and real time monitoring.
- Meet the supply with the demand for water to efficiently distribute water throughout the distribution lines.
- With the smart water sensors installed at various points in the distribution lines, monitor and control the quality of water.

Biz4Intellia provides smart water distribution by embedding water sensors in the pipelines to monitor the flow and direction of water. *Biz4Intellia's* IoT solution for water industry can also notify water distributors about any leakage in the pipeline. The key benefit of implementing IoT water solution is that it can notify water distributors about any leakages in the pipelines. *Biz4Intellia IoT* smart water solution is enabling the intelligent use of water at home, in the fields, and across cities [126].

By handling problems in creative ways, using simple and increasingly inexpensive technologies, you can reduce water wastage and keep waterways clean. As urbanization and growing population demands more from the water supply, the IoT smart water solutions make the optimum water supply to conserve this precious resource for future generations.

2.8 IoT FOR AFFORDABLE AND CLEAN ENERGY

The future hope of the energy sector is smart grid. The IoT has an important role in making the smart grid an efficient system [126]. The power usage data is generated by the individual appliance and is aggregated at smart meters towards end-user. This data is communicated to the utility cente; and based on the utility-decision, the power usage is systematically planned. All the information communication and controlling of the data is happening through the IoT [127].

Also, using the IoT for smart grid applications has a great impact on energy management. Based on the data generated, the smart grid can make efficient decisions on switching the energy between the renewable and conventional energy resources. IoT also manages the individual's power plan efficiently [128]. This planning not only decreases the power bills of the user but also the decreases the load on the grid [129].

IoT-based energy management is very important in decreasing the faults occurring [130]. With the introduction of IoT, power theft can be identified easily; this increases the system stability [131]. The efficient home automation using the IoT increases the luxury and the living standards of the users [132].

2.9 IoT FOR SUSTAINABLE CITIES AND COMMUNITIES

The applications of the IoT are becoming very resourceful, from controlling an individual appliance to a larger system like smart grid or smart cities [133]. The integration of the many smart systems into a hub making all the devices connected is the vision of many advanced countries for the near future [134]. The interconnection of the many smart devices that are using IoT ensure better services for urban areas [135]. Traffic management is the most important problem faced by almost all the cities in this world; this issue can be efficiently addressed by the IoT-based smart city concept. The urban water supply problem can also be addressed systematically. The municipal waste management and the drainage maintenance can also be handled in an efficient manner. City surveillance, weather monitoring, traffic monitoring, and parking lot maintenance are useful ideas for smart cities in connection to the IoT concept [136].

REFERENCES

1. https://www.un.org/sustainabledevelopment/ (accessed June 5, 2019).
2. http://widgets.weforum.org/iot4d/ (accessed June 5, 2019).
3. J. Simon Elias Bibri. 2018. The IoT for Smart Sustainable Cities of the Future: An Analytical Framework for Sensor-based Big Data Applications for Environmental Sustainability. *Sustainable Cities and Society.* 38: 230–253.
4. https://wir2018.wid.world/ (accessed June 5, 2019).
5. https://www.unfpa.org/resources/population-and-poverty (accessed June 5, 2019).
6. https://www.statista.com/chart/11963/the-most-and-least-expensive-countries-for-broadband/ (accessed June 5, 2019).
7. https://www.worldbank.org/en/news/press-release/2018/02/26/world-bank-group-and-gsma-announce-partnership-to-leverage-iot-big-data-for-development (accessed June 5, 2019).
8. http://unglobalpulse.org/sites/default/files/MobileDataforSocialGoodReport_29June.pdf (accessed June 5, 2019).
9. https://uidai.gov.in/ (accessed June 5, 2019).
10. https://www.nadra.gov.pk/ (accessed June 5, 2019).
11. Money channel distribution case – Kenya. https://www.ifc.org/wps/wcm/connect/4e64a80049585fd9a13ab519583b6d16/tool+6.7.+case+study+-+m-pesa+kenya+.pdf?mod=ajpcres (accessed June 5, 2019).
12. https://coinfrenzy.io/alipay-chinese-govt-partnership/ (accessed June 5, 2019).
13. https://www.easypaisa.com.pk/ (accessed June 5, 2019).
14. https://dbtbharat.gov.in/ (accessed June 5, 2019).
15. Linda Hultberg. 2008. *Women Empowerment in Bangladesh A Study of the Village Pay Phone Program*, C-thesis. Jonkoping University, Media and Communication Studies.
16. https://www.unglobalpulse.org/ (accessed June 5, 2019).
17. http://www.pmindia.gov.in/en/mann-ki-baat/ (accessed June 5, 2019).
18. http://www.ict.go.ke/ (accessed June 5, 2019).
19. http://www.burmalibrary.org/docs23/2013-10-08-Telecommunications_Law-en.pdf (accessed June 5, 2019).
20. A.R. Al-Ali, Conf. 2016. Internet of Things Role in Renewable Energy Resources. Presented in 3rd International Conference on Power and Energy Systems Engineering, CPESE 2016. *Energy Procedia.* 100: 34–38.

21. https://www.gsma.com/iot/wp-content/uploads/2018/02/iot_clean_air_02_18.pdf (accessed June 5, 2019).
22. https://www.unocha.org/story/philippines-typhoon-haiyan-and-digital-last-mile (accessed June 5, 2019).
23. https://www.ericsson.com/ourportfolio/network-solutions/massive-iot (accessed June 5, 2019).
24. https://www.zte.com.cn/china/topics/ztepre5g_en/field-massive.html (accessed June 5, 2019).
25. https://farmappweb.com/ (accessed June 5, 2019).
26. http://growlink.com/ (accessed June 5, 2019).
27. https://easternpeak.com/works/iot/ (accessed June 5, 2019).
28. https://arable.com/ (accessed June 5, 2019).
29. https://semios.com/ (accessed June 5, 2019).
30. https://www.allmeteo.com/ (accessed June 5, 2019).
31. https://smartelements.io/ (accessed June 5, 2019).
32. https://www.pycno.co/ (accessed June 5, 2019).
33. http://www.scrdairy.com/ (accessed June 5, 2019).
34. https://www.cowlar.com/ (accessed June 5, 2019).
35. http://www.technologyrecord.com/Article/cojengo-develops-vetafrica-app-to-help-farmers-expedite-livestock-diagnosis-40016 (accessed June 5, 2019).
36. http://www.fao.org/3/CA1078EN/ca1078en.pdf (accessed June 5, 2019).
37. https://farmlogs.com/ (accessed June 5, 2019).
38. https://about.cropio.com/#cropio (accessed June 5, 2019).
39. https://www.agrivi.com/farm-management (accessed June 5, 2019).
40. https://conservis.ag/ (accessed June 5, 2019).
41. http://www.fujitsu.com/global/about/resources/case-studies/cs-2016oct-iwata-smart-agriculture.html (accessed June 5, 2019).
42. http://www.sharp-world.com/corporate/news/130920.html (accessed June 5, 2019).
43. https://uponics.com/panasonic-vertical-farming/ (accessed June 5, 2019).
44. https://inhabitat.com/toshibas-clean-factory-farm-produces-3-million-bags-of-lettuce-a-year-without-sunlight-or-soil/ (accessed June 5, 2019).
45. https://www.ericsson.com/ourportfolio/iot-solution-areas/iot-accelerator (accessed June 5, 2019).
46. http://www.fao.org/giews/en/ (accessed June 5, 2019).
47. http://www.fao.org/ag/locusts/en/activ/DLIS/dailyphotos/index.html (accessed June 5, 2019).
48. http://www.amis-outlook.org/ (accessed June 5, 2019).
49. http://www.fao.org/3/a-i5564e.pdf (accessed June 5, 2019).
50. http://www.icow.co.ke/ (accessed June 5, 2019).
51. http://mfarm.co.ke/ (accessed June 5, 2019).

52. https://www.esoko.com/ (accessed June 5, 2019).
53. http://www.agro-hub.com/ (accessed June 5, 2019).
54. https://www.worldcocoafoundation.org/cocoa-updates/ (accessed June 5, 2019).
55. https://kilimosalama.files.wordpress.com/2010/02/kilimo-salama-fact-sheet-final11.pdf (accessed June 5, 2019).
56. http://www.bbc.com/future/story/20120816-a-farm-in-your-backpack (accessed June 5, 2019).
57. https://www.modisar.com/ (accessed June 5, 2019).
58. https://www.grandviewresearch.com/press-release/global-iot-in-healthcare-market (accessed June 5, 2019).
59. https://www.technavio.com/report/global-it-professional-services-internet-things-market-healthcare-sector-market (accessed June 5, 2019).
60. https://guardtime.com/blog/estonian-ehealth-partners-guardtime-blockchain-based-transparency (accessed June 5, 2019).
61. Sanjay Sareen, Sandeep K. Sood, Sunil Kumar Gupta. 2018. IoT-Based Cloud Framework to Control Ebola Virus Outbreak. *Journal of Ambient Intelligence and Humanized Computing.* 9(3): 459–476, June.
62. Sanjay Sareen, Sandeep K Sood, Sunil Kumar Gupta. 2017. SecureIoT-based Cloud Framework to Control Zika Virus Outbreak. *International Journal of Technology Assessment in Health Care.* 33(1): 1–8, April.
63. Rajinder Sandhu, Harsuminder Kaur Gill, J. Sandeep Sood. 2015. Smart Monitoring and Controlling of Pandemic Influenza A (H1N1) Using Social Network Analysis and Cloud Computing. *Journal of Computational Science.* 12(C): 11–22.
64. https://controlant.com/industries/pharmaceuticals/ (accessed June 5, 2019).
65. https://www.ericsson.com/en/internet-of-things/cases (accessed June 5, 2019).
66. https://cdn.ymaws.com/echalliance.com/resource/resmgr/Docs/DHWS16/10003_FLORENCE_GAUDRY-PERKI.pdf (accessed June 5, 2019).
67. Andrew Lippman, J. Nchinda Nchinda, Kallirroi Retzepi. 2018. MedRec: Patient Control of Medical Record Distribution. *IEEE Blockchain Newsletter.*
68. https://www.healthcaretechnologies.com/using-the-internet-of-things-for-vaccine-supply-chain (accessed June 5, 2019).
69. https://thepump.jsi.com/using-the-internet-of-things-to-manage-vaccines-and-save-lives-in-tanzania/ (accessed June 5, 2019).
70. https://ihub.co.ke/ (accessed June 5, 2019).
71. https://www.medsc.org/pdfs/2017FallImprovingOperationsDeliveryCare.pdf (accessed June 5, 2019).

72. https://www.digitalistmag.com/tag/rths (accessed June 5, 2019).
73. Y. Cai, X.Q. Huang, J. He. 2012. High-Voltage Equipment Monitoring System Based on IOT. In: P. Senac, M. Ott, A. Seneviratne, (eds) *Wireless Communications and Applications. ICWCA 2011. Lecture Notes of the Institute for Computer Sciences,* 72. Springer, Berlin, Heidelberg, 2011.
74. https://www.automationworld.com/article/technologies/security/ equipment-monitoring-software-iot (accessed June 5, 2019).
75. M. Yaseen, D. Swathi, T.A. Kumar. 2017. IoT Based Condition Monitoring of Generators and Predictive Maintenance. *2017 2nd International Conference on Communication and Electronics Systems (ICCES), Coimbatore.* 725–729. Oct 2017.
76. https://www.ihris.org/ (accessed June 5, 2019).
77. http://www.who.int/hinari/en/ (accessed June 5, 2019).
78. https://humanhealth.iaea.org/hhw/ (accessed June 5, 2019).
79. https://humanhealth.iaea.org/HHW/NuclearMedicine/DATOL/ English/index.html (accessed June 5, 2019).
80. https://cancer.iaea.org/vuccnet.asp (accessed June 5, 2019).
81. https://play.google.com/store/apps/details?id=com.app. tnm&hl=en_IN (accessed June 5, 2019).
82. https://itunes.apple.com/us/app/tnm/id1039644483?mt=8 (accessed June 5, 2019).
83. https://play.google.com/store/apps/details?id=app.com. figostaging&hl=en_IN (accessed June 5, 2019).
84. https://itunes.apple.com/us/app/figo-gyn-cancer-management/ id1153038788?mt=8 (accessed June 5, 2019).
85. https://play.google.com/store/apps/details?id=it.tecnoconference. aimn&hl=en_IN (accessed June 5, 2019).
86. https://itunes.apple.com/us/app/nucard/id1153488902?mt=8 (accessed June 5, 2019).
87. http://elearning.iaea.org/m2/course/index.php?categoryid=114 (accessed June 5, 2019).
88. https://www.igniteengineers.com/mooc-advantages-and-disadvan- tages/ (accessed June 5, 2019).
89. Sang-Yong Tom Lee, Hee-Woong Kim, Sumeet Gupta. 2007. Measuring Open Source Software Success. *Omega.* 37: 426–438.
90. http://worldslargestlesson.globalgoals.org/ (accessed June 5, 2019).
91. http://unesdoc.unesco.org/images/0021/002134/213475e.pdf (accessed June 5, 2019).
92. Maribel Burrola Vasqueza, J. Jose Angel Vera Noriega. 2013. Study about ICT Skills in Junior High School Teachers under Mexico's Educational Reform. *International Journal of Psychological Research.* 2: 59–70.
93. Mary Hooker, Esther Mwiyeria, Anubha Verma. 2011. ICT Competency Framework for Teachers in Nigeria-Report.

94. Higher Education Report, Pakistan. http://hec.gov.pk/english/services/universities/RevisedCurricula/Documents/2011-2012/Education/ICTsEdu_Sept13.pdf (accessed June 5, 2019).

95. http://www.education2030-africa.org/images/talent/atelier_normes/En-20_Cadre_curriculaire_commun_Formation_des_enseignants.pdf – June 2016 (accessed June 5, 2019).

96. https://en.unesco.org/events/unesco-china-funds-trust-project-harnessing-technology-quality-teacher-training-africa-phase (accessed June 5, 2019).

97. https://bangkok.unesco.org/content/transforming-myanmar-rural-schools-ict-one-teacher-time (accessed June 5, 2019).

98. https://jaago.com.bd/ (accessed June 5, 2019).

99. https://jo-moe.openemis.org/portal/(accessed June 5, 2019).

100. https://kiron.ngo/ (accessed June 5, 2019).

101. https://www.warchildholland.org/cant-wait-to-learn (accessed June 5, 2019).

102. https://ureport.in/ (accessed June 5, 2019).

103. https://educationinnovations.org/program/edutrac-peru (accessed June 5, 2019).

104. http://ehub.co.za/ (accessed June 5, 2019).

105. http://connecttolearn.org (accessed June 5, 2019).

106. https://www.unglobalpulse.org/sites/default/files/Gender-equality-and-big-data-en-2018.pdf (accessed June 5, 2019).

107. https://welearn.unwomen.org/ (accessed June 5, 2019).

108. https://www.heforshe.org/en/impact (accessed June 5, 2019).

109. https://www.empowerwomen.org/en/campaigns/herstory (accessed June 5, 2019).

110. http://www.fao.org/tempref/docrep/fao/004/y1931m/y1931m04.pdf (accessed June 5, 2019).

111. http://www.fao.org/3/a-y4312e.pdf (accessed June 5, 2019).

112. https://www.swiggy.com/delhi/million-kitchen-00-hauz-khas (accessed June 5, 2019).

113. http://homefoodies.pk/ (accessed June 5, 2019).

114. https://girlsgoit.org/ (accessed June 5, 2019).

115. https://learning.mozilla.org/en-US/clubs/about (accessed June 5, 2019).

116. http://www.unwomen.org/en/news/stories/2018/10/feature-empow-ering-women-farmers-in-rwanda (accessed June 5, 2019).

117. http://unesdoc.unesco.org/images/0022/002269/226903e.pdf (accessed June 5, 2019).

118. http://stemcenter.gsnetx.org/ (accessed June 5, 2019).

119. http://connecttolearn.org (accessed June 5, 2019).

120. Enhancing Women Empowerment through Information and Communication Technology, A Report, Submitted to Department of Women & Child Development Ministry of HRD Government of India by Voluntary Association For People Service (VAPS). Training and Research Centre, Madurai.

121. E. Jane, J. Fountain. 2000. Constructing the Information Society: Women, Information Technology, and Design. *Technology in Society*. 22(1): 45–62.
122. http://www.wcd.nic.in/schemes-listing/2405 (accessed June 5, 2019).
123. https://ewater.org.au/ (accessed June 5, 2019).
124. http://www.mobiloitte.com/blog/driving-digital-transformation-smart-cities-iot-prospects-challenges (accessed June 5, 2019).
125. http://developer.huawei.com/ict/en/site-iot/article/liteos-smart-meter (accessed June 5, 2019).
126. http://www.biz4intellia.com/blog/iot-in-water-water-conservation-for-future-generation/ (accessed June 5, 2019).
127. S. Sofana Reka, J. Tomislav Dragicevic. 2018. Future Effectual Role of Energy Delivery: A Comprehensive Review of Internet of Things and Smart Grid. *Renewable and Sustainable Energy Reviews*. 91: 90–108.
128. K. Vikram, J. Sarat Kumar Sahoo. 2017. Load Aware Channel Estimation and Channel Scheduling for 2.4GHz Frequency Band Wireless Networks for Smart Grid Applications. *International Journal on Smart Sensing and Intelligent Systems*. 10(4): 879–902.
129. K. Vikram, J. Sarat Kumar Sahoo. 2018. A Collaborative Frame Work for Avoiding the Interference in 2.4GHz Frequency Band Smart Grid Applications. *Faculty of Electrical Engineering Banja Luka, Electronics Journal*. 22(1): 48–56.
130. K. Vikram, J. Venkata Lakshmi Narayana. 2015. A Survey on Wireless Sensor Networks for Smart Grid. *Sensors & Transducers Journal*. 186(3): 18–24.
131. K. Vikram, Sarat Kumar Sahoo. 2018. Chapter 9 – Energy Management System in Smart Grid. In *Smart Grid Systems-Modelling and Control*. CRC Press, Taylor & Francis Group. 1, 224–254. ISBN 9781771886253.
132. K. Vikram, K. Sarat Kumar Sahoo, J. Venkata Lakshmi Narayana. 2017. Forward Error Correction based Encoding Technique for Cross-layer Multi Channel MAC Protocol. *Energy Procedia*. 117: 847–854.
133. M. Mohammadi, A. Al-Fuqaha, M. Guizani, J. Oh. 2018. Semisupervised Deep Reinforcement Learning in Support of IoT and Smart City Services. *IEEE Internet of Things Journal*. 5(2): 624–635.
134. B. Ahlgren, M. Hidell E. C. J. Ngai. 2016. Internet of Things for Smart Cities: Interoperability and Open Data. *IEEE Internet Computing*. 20(6): 52–56.

135. K. Vikram, K. V. L. Narayana. 2016. Cross-layer Multi Channel MAC Protocol for Wireless Sensor Networks in 2.4GHz ISM Band. *International Conference on Computing, Analytics and Security Trends (CAST)*, Pune. 312–317.
136. C. A. Kamienski, F. F. Borelli, G. O. Biondi, I. Pinheiro, I. D. Zyrianoff M. J. Jentsch. 2018. Context Design and Tracking for IoT-based Energy Management in Smart Cities. *IEEE Internet of Things Journal*. 5(2): 687–695.

3

SMARTPHONE CROWD COMPUTING: A RATIONAL APPROACH FOR SUSTAINABLE COMPUTING BY CURBING THE ENVIRONMENTAL EXTERNALITIES OF THE GROWING COMPUTING DEMANDS

Pijush Kanti Dutta Pramanik, Saurabh Pal,
and Prasenjit Choudhury

CONTENTS

3.1 INTRODUCTION

In the year 2017, the U.S. was hit by several devastating natural disasters that ranged from floods and hurricanes to droughts and wildfires. Let us take a look at some of them, which caused major damage and indicate the operation of the environment (Climatenexus 2018):

- **Hurricanes Irma, Harvey, and Maria:** The U.S. was hit by three Category 4 hurricanes during 2017. The storm and the accompanying rainfall led to an unprecedented rise in the sea level, resulting in a devastating flood. Hurricane Harvey was fuelled by record-breaking rainfall (reportedly, 1-in-25,000 year rain).
- **Atmospheric river storms in California:** Throughout the winter season of 2017, different parts of California were hit by several back-to-back extreme atmospheric river storms that produced record rainfall and flooding in the state.
- **Spring snow/rainfall and floods:** In mid-March, the Northeastern U.S. received snowfall at an astonishing rate of 7 inches per hour totalling to 42 inches, thanks to the winter storm Stella. In late-April, the Midwestern U.S. was devastatingly flooded due to heavy rainfall of up to 15 inches. The percentage of heaviest 1% of rainy and snowy days has been increased by 53 and 92 in the Midwestern and the Northeastern U.S. respectively during the years 1958 through 2016.

- **High plains flash drought:** In July, flash drought gripped the Dakotas and Montana, which led to one of Montana's worst wildfires, causing agricultural losses of $2.5 billion.
- **California experienced a record heat:** On September 1, the temperature in San Francisco reached 106°F, breaking its all-time heat record. Actually, from late August through early September, the whole of California experienced the worst state-wide heat wave ever recorded, and many parts of it broke daily, monthly, and all-time temperature records. In fact, heat waves have become more frequent across the U.S.
- **Plains on fire:** A few weeks after the record heat wave in September, California was hit by the deadliest and most destructive fires in state history, killing 40 people and destroying a total of 8,323 structures. Earlier, around March, places like Kansas, Oklahoma, Colorado, and Texas were blazed by major fires. The fire of Oklahoma was the largest wildfire on record in the state, breaking the previous record just set one year prior. These fires are not one-off incidents. The wildfire incidents are consistently increasing over the years in the western U.S. grasslands or the Great Plains region. Since the 1970s, in every decade, more than 100,000 acres of extra grass and shrubland caught fire than the previous decade. In a study covering over three-decade period (1984–2014), it is observed that the total area burned by large wildfires in the Great Plains rose by 400%.
- **Summer in winter:** Generally, if the ratio of days that record the highest temperature and the days that of lowest temperature is evenly balanced, the climate is supposed to be stable. But for the past three decades, the balance has been disrupted. Due to the consistently warm climate, the number of record high-temperature days have begun to outpace the number of record low-temperature days. In the month of February, there were 34 instances of heat-record breaking for every cold-record breaking in different parts of the U.S. As a result of this growing imbalance, February was one of Chicago's warmest on record.
- **Reduced snowing in winter:** Chicago had the least snow cover during the months of January and February since 1884. This is attributed mainly to the unseasonably and atypical warm and rainy weather. The climate change caused a significant reduction in snow cover extent over high northern latitudes during the last 100 years.

These environmental idiosyncrasies are not limited only to the U.S. The impact of the changing environment and climate is being experienced worldwide and, on many occasions, severely. The effect ranges from Antarctic glacier melting to the expansion of the Sahara Desert. Why these abnormal behaviours of nature? Is there any common and explainable reason behind this? Yes, the culprit is very real and obvious—global warming. Let us try to understand, tersely, the effect of warm weather in the contexts of the above-mentioned events.

Hurricanes are heat engines that are fuelled by warm tropical waters. The warm seas increase the potential energy available to passing storms over them, thus swelling the power and speed of these cyclones, converting them into deadly hurricanes. For instance, the Gulf of Mexico was 7°F warmer than the average temperature (over the period between 1961 and 1990) which stimulated Hurricane Harvey. A warmer atmosphere holds and dumps more moisture, which increases the precipitation level substantially, resulting in heavy rainfall. The heavily moist atmosphere is also the reason for extreme snowfall. On the other hand, flash droughts are driven by rapidly decreasing soil moisture because of increased temperatures and lack of precipitation in the air. The extreme heat was the reason for July's drought in the High Plains areas. Similarly, studies have established global warming as the key reason for the unusual heat that swept across the U.S. as well as diminished snowfall in some parts of the U.S. This high temperature along with the abrupt variability in the dry and wet weather conditions boost chances of wildfire by increasing the abundance and dryness of available fuel.

The phenomenon of global warming and climate change is largely man-made and has been accelerating at a rapid and unprecedented way since the Industrial Revolution began in the late 1700s (Pramanik, Mukherjee, Pal, Upadhyaya et al. 2019). According to NASA, since 1880, the average temperature of the Earth has risen 0.8°C which is projected to increase further, according to the U.S. Environmental Protection Agency (EPA), between 1.13 and 6.42°C over the next 100 years.

The main reason for the warming of the Earth is the greenhouse gas effect that obstructs the infrared and heat radiation to escape from Earth toward space. Gases that contribute most to the greenhouse effect include water vapour, carbon dioxide (CO_2), methane, nitrous oxide (N_2O), chlorofluorocarbons (CFCs), etc. Most of these gases are human-produced and are responsible for increasing the Earth's temperature over the past 50 years. Among these, CO_2 is the most common greenhouse gas in the atmosphere. For instance, in 2012, CO_2 reportedly accounted for nearly 82% of all greenhouse gas emissions in the U.S. In the last 150 years, mainly due to the industrial activities, the atmospheric CO_2 levels are raised from 280 ppm (parts per million) to 410 ppm, which is further expected to be degraded to 450 ppm by 2035 unless greenhouse gas emissions are controlled strictly (R. Monroe 2016).

Electricity generation is one of the major sources of carbon pollution, because in most countries, still today, the majority of the electricity is generated by burning fossil fuels. For example, even a developed nation like Australia gets 73% and 13% of its electricity by burning coal and gas, respectively (WWF-Australia 2018). Besides other industries, the rapid advancement of the ICT industry (that includes computers and peripherals, computer and telecommunication networks and associated equipment, and the data centres) has soared the energy consumption like never before. At present, globally, nearly 10% of the total energy is consumed by the ICT industry. Factually, the total global energy demand is estimated at 20,000 TWh, whereas IT is accountable for using 2,000 TWh (Jones 2018). This huge energy consumption produces roughly 1.7% (530 Mt) of the total CO_2 emissions (Gelenbe and Caseau 2015). ICT's carbon footprint is roughly equal to the carbon emission from the aviation industry's fuel burning. Experiencing the ultra-penetration of ICT into every sphere of human life that results in increased energy consumption rate by 20% per year, it is expected that the world's energy consumption of ICT will be double by 2030. Out of total energy consumption by ICT, two-thirds are attributed to the devices, data centres while the rest goes for the telecommunication networks.

The negative environmental externalities of ICT can be reduced to some extent if the production and usage of computers are checked. But this is not feasible. On the other side, smartphones have become indispensable these days, and day-by-day, they are becoming computationally powerful. It is proposed that if these abundantly available smartphones are utilised as computing resources, it will allow getting away with the unnecessary production of desktops and laptops. Additionally, due to the much smaller size, production of smartphones will yield much lesser environment hazards. Therefore, using smartphones for computations is assessed to be a feasible solution for catering the demand of ever-growing computation needs while minimizing the environmental hazards. Furthermore, a number of such powerful smartphone devices, collectively, can offer huge computing capability. A satisfactory high-performance computing (HPC) may be achieved by making a grid of smartphones (Pramanik, Choudhury and Saha, 2017) (Pramanik, Pal and Pareek et al. 2018). The cumulative computing power achieved by such grids of smartphones can tail off the dependency on the data centres and low-end supercomputers as well. Since in this proposed computing environment, the public owned smartphones are targeted to be utilised, this particular computing system is named as smartphone crowd computing (SCC).

In this chapter, the negative impacts of ICT are discussed in minute detail. The emphasis is given on sustainable computing and different means to achieve it. And finally, a special discussion is presented on SCC and how SCC can help to achieve sustainable computing goal.

The rest of the chapter is organized as follows. Section 3.2 discusses the environmental threats caused by ICT. Section 3.3 discusses the basics of sustainable computing in terms of environmental issues. Section 3.4 suggests actions should be followed by organizations to achieve sustainable computing. Section 3.5 mentions general solutions, in terms of computation, that can help in low energy consumption of computing and storage devices. Different computing approaches for achieving sustainable computing are discussed in Section 3.6. Section 3.7 suggests the role of smartphone crowd computing in sustainable computing. Section 3.8 concludes the chapter.

3.2 ENVIRONMENTAL EXTERNALITIES OF ICT

3.2.1 Externality

An externality, generally used in the context of economics, refers to the impact of an activity that affects an unrelated third party. Depending on the beneficial or adverse impact, the externality is termed as a positive externality or negative externality. The problem with the externalities is that they generally don't affect the causer (the company/organization) directly, especially economically. Also, in most of the cases, they cannot be held accountable for the damage, legally. Hence, they (the causer) generally do not bother to address the issues. Barry Commoner, one of the leading ecologists ever and a pioneer of the modern environmental movement, commented on the costs of externalities long back, which is still crucially relevant (Commoner 1969):

> Clearly, we have compiled a record of serious failures in recent technological encounters with the environment. In each case, the new technology was brought into use before the ultimate hazards were known. We have been quick to reap the benefits and slow to comprehend the costs.

3.2.2 Environmental Externalities in General

An environmental externality is typically implied as a negative externality that is common for any industry in the context of environmental economics. In industrial terms, the environmental externality is caused by the process of the production or the consumption of goods or services. Though the environmental externality has a serious consequence to the society in general, the organizations do not care to be concerned, mainly due to economic, technical, and infrastructural overheads. Some of the examples of environmental externalities are:

- Air pollution, largely due to the massive use of fossil fuels (vehicles and industry), burning leftover corps on the fields, wildfires, etc., which damages public health, biodiversity, crops, architecture (e.g., historic buildings and monuments), and almost everything in the world.
- Water pollution, mainly due to industrial wastes, which harms every living element in the planet that depends on water.
- Noise pollution, from various sources, affects birds, animals, and especially humans, disrupting the mental and psychological health.
- Greenhouse gas emissions, caused by burning fossil fuels and cultivating livestock, which is expediting the anthropogenic climate change.

3.2.3 The Negative Externalities of ICT in Terms of Environmental Sustainability

The growing demand for ICT has reasoned for the overwhelming production of ICT products. People are using, changing, or upgrading their devices like never before. The following reasons are attributed to the enormous increase in e-devices (Honda, Khetriwal and Kuehr 2016):

- **More gadgets:** The continuous advancement in electronics and allied technologies, along with people's changing lifestyles, is driving the innovation and the introduction of new products, regularly.
- **More consumers:** More affordability due to the reduced price of electronic products and growing a middle-class segment among the already swelling population; especially in the East and the South-East Asian region, the number of consumers has soared up.

- **Decreasing usage cycle:** The average usage cycle of electronic gadgets has considerably decreased, for which the credit goes to both consumers and manufacturers. The companies are consciously and tactfully decreasing the device operation cycles by introducing new products persistently and making the older (not too old) hardware and software incompatible with new applications. Consumers are also falling for this trap, switching to new gadgets more swiftly than required, be it for passion or fashion.
- **More availability:** The open market in global business has eased the import of electronic products to the demanding countries, making the products (both new and second-hand) more available.

The production and use of these ICT products have triggered several negative externalities related to the environment. The negative externalities of growing computing devices are discussed in the following.

Use of natural resources: Use of natural resources in the production of the ICT products is a reason for natural resource depletion from the Earth; thus, unbalancing the natural diversity. To back this argument, let us check out the following statistics (United Nations University Newsletter 2004):

- The amount (in terms of weight) of fossil fuel and chemicals required in manufacturing an average desktop computer is at least 10 times its own weight. This ratio is much more than in the case of an automobile or refrigerator, which require fossil fuel amounts 1–2 times their weight.
- In the process of producing one desktop computer with a 17-inch CRT monitor, at least 240 kg of fossil fuels, 22 kg of chemicals, and 1,500 kg of water are needed, which accounts a total material of 1.8 tons.

Energy consumption: Device production and operations consume huge energy. For example, nearly 30,000 megajoules of energy is used in the manufacturing of an average computer. The energy consumption demands more energy production, which increases the carbon footprint (Pramanik, Mukherjee, Pal, Pal et al. 2019).

Effects of the manufacturing process: The production of computer hardware causes pollution havoc. The different parts of a computer and its peripherals contain several harmful heavy metals.

Along with the environment, these toxic heavy metals are very dangerous to human and animal health. Long-term exposure to these elements may be fatal to the workers and their families, and also the neighbouring communities. Some of the most hazardous metals that damagingly effect hominoid health are:

- Antimony (Sb): Immediate contact with antimony may cause aggravated irritation of the eyes, skin, and lungs. Long-term exposure to this toxic metal can cause stomach pain, diarrhoea, vomiting, stomach ulcers, pulmonary edema (swelling due to the accumulation of interstitial fluid in an organ or any area of the body), chronic bronchitis, chronic obstructive pulmonary disease (COPD, includes both chronic bronchitis and emphysema), pneumoconiosis, altered electrocardiograms, spontaneous abortion, and menstrual irregularities.
- Arsenic (As): Arsenic is one of the most toxic metals found in the Earth's ground. It has severe impacts on human health. Long-term exposure to high levels of arsenic is highly cancerous and is one of the main reasons for skin, bladder, and lung cancer. Arsenic is also associated with heart disease. Small amounts (<5 mg) of arsenic ingestion (through water or pesticides/insecticides) cause nausea, vomiting, abdominal pain, and diarrhoea. Acute poisoning due to a lethal dose of arsenic (100 mg to 300 mg) may lead to death.
- Beryllium (Be): Exposure to beryllium fumes and particles causes chronic beryllium disease (a fatal respiratory disease). Beryllium also has the potential to harm different organs like the liver, kidneys, heart, and nervous system. This carcinogen metal may cause lung cancer also.
- Cadmium (Cd): Cadmium is a highly toxic element, and if inhaled at excessive levels, it can cause death. Long-term exposure to cadmium can damage kidneys and bones. Excessive exposure may harm lung function and increase the risk of lung cancer.
- Chromium (Cr): Chromium compounds affect the respiratory tract badly, resulting in diseases like asthma, chronic bronchitis, chronic irritation, chronic pharyngitis, chronic rhinitis, congestion and hyperaemia, polyps of the upper respiratory tract, tracheobronchitis, etc. High dose of chromium exposure may even lead to lung, nasal, or sinus

cancers. Cases of sperm damage and the male reproductive system also been observed as a result of chromium exposure.

- Cobalt (Co): Though cobalt is beneficial for humans because it is a metal constituent of vitamin B12, high concentrations of cobalt may promote various adverse health effects. High concentrations of cobalt may affect human health, causing vomiting and nausea, vision problems, heart problems, and thyroid damage. As per clinical experiments, cobalt has also been classified to be carcinogenic.
- Lead (Pb): Lead affects the kidneys and reproductive systems. Even low levels of lead can be harmful to a child's nervous system and mental development.
- Mercury (Hg): Mercury is linked to brain and kidney damage. It also affects the nervous, digestive, and immune systems. Mercury is seriously harmful to the developing fetus and young children, affecting the nervous and cognitive system.
- Selenium (Se): Selenium is known to have many benefits (mainly due to its antioxidant properties) to human health if it is consumed at a moderate level. But a high dose of it has several adverse health effects. Overexposure of selenium may cause an accumulation of fluid in the lungs. Selenium is also attributed to health menaces like bad breath, bronchitis, bronchial asthma, shortness of breath, nausea, vomiting, abdominal pain, diarrhoea, enlarged liver, conjunctivitis, and pneumonitis. High concentrations of selenium are associated with skin cancer, prostate cancer, and diabetes. High enough levels of selenium can be the cause of death.

In addition to the above-mentioned, other metals such as aluminium (Al), barium (Ba), copper (Cu), gallium (Ga), gold (Au), iron (Fe), manganese (Mn), palladium (Pd), platinum (Pt), silver (Ag), and zinc (Zn) are also used in manufacturing a PC. Exposure to these metals at considerable amounts is harmful to organisms.

The chemicals involved in the production of computers also damage the environment and the health of living beings. For example, nitrogen trifluoride (NF_3), used in liquid crystal display (LCD), thin-film photovoltaic cells and microcircuit manufacturing, has 17,000 times greater potential to cause global warming as compared to CO_2 (R. Monroe 2008). Brominated flame retardant (BFR), another important substance used in computer production, may lead to thyroid damage and undeveloped fetus.

The oil-based paints that are used for the finished products are also extremely toxic in nature. All of these metals and chemicals and toxic materials cause water contamination and air pollution, damaging the global environment.

Burden of hazardous e-waste: We are experiencing an e-waste tsunami. E-waste, one of the fastest-growing types of waste worldwide, has become a serious threat to the Earth. Globally, in 2014, the per inhabitant e-waste generation was recorded as 5.8 kg, which increased to 6.3 kg in 2017 and is expected to reach 7.0 kg by 2022 (Research and Markets 2019) (Honda, Khetriwal and Kuehr 2016). Worldwide, 20 to 50 million tons of e-waste are generated every year (Leblanc, E-Waste Recycling Facts and Figures 2018a).

The increase in production and buying of computing devices, along with changing technology, has seriously contributed to increasing electronic waste. Thanks to the very regular launch of new products, consumers now tend to upgrade/replace their device more frequently. The replacement cycle for PCs is 3–4 years. As a matter of fact, approximately 90% of the discarded computer accessories are not recycled but dumped openly.

Among the total solid waste deposited in landfills, 70% of the hazardous waste is accounted to e-waste (Leblanc, E-Waste Recycling Facts and Figures 2018a). This huge amount of e-waste releases a substantial amount of toxic materials, volatile organic chemicals, and heavy metals which not only exhaust resources but cause environmental pollution and global climate change. The toxic elements due to improper waste disposal pollute the soil, making it infertile and unable to support crops and other plant life (Gillespie 2018). This deters the production of foods, which eventually leads to malnourishment of the natives and the nationals. Furthermore, the contaminated food farmed on the polluted soil may be the source of serious illness.

Often, the e-wastes are sent to developing countries to be dumped in landfills. People extract valuable materials such as gold, silver, and copper from the discarded electronics by burning the substances. This produces hazardous gas and smoke (due to the presence of other toxic materials) by which not only the air but water also gets polluted. This is not only the case of the developing countries but in developed countries also; the consumers and the persons/organizations responsible for dismantling and recycling the e-waste often illegally dump these on the open areas.

There are various reasons for people not following the proper procedures of decomposing the e-waste. Some of them are (Honda, Khetriwal and Kuehr 2016):

- **Lack of awareness:** In the majority of the cases, the users are not informed of the fact that they should dispose of the electronic device systematically once it is obsolete/discarded. Even if they are aware of this, they do not know how or where to dispose of their e-waste. On the other hand, the untrained and ignorant recyclers may fail the purpose of recycling by not following standard procedures.
- **Insufficient incentives:** If the users have to pay for disposing the e-waste to the recycling or waste-collection system, they prefer not to do so.
- **Inconvenience:** Even if the disposal of e-waste to the recycling or waste-collection system is free, users may be discouraged in disposing of their e-waste properly due to inept disposal system and inconvenient procedure and avenue which eats up their time and effort.
- **Dearth of suitable dumping sites:** Not having enough proper dumping locations, especially in the largely populated cities may be a critical hurdle for e-waste disposal.
- **Weak governance with flaccid rule enforcement:** A country that has ineffectual or no policy and legislation enforcement for e-waste regulation violation may result in rampant non-compliance. Governments, civic bodies, and industries have important roles to play in tackling the e-waste management problem. The general responsibilities of governments and industries are listed in Figure 3.1 and Figure 3.2, respectively.

Industrial discharge: Untreated industrial discharges like oil, toxic chemicals, and sewage contaminate the water bodies like rivers and lakes. The polluted water is dangerous for aquatic creatures. For instance, over 8,000 marine lives were reported dead six months after the disastrous *Deepwater Horizon* oil spill in 2010 that affected 16,000 miles of U.S. coastline (Gillespie 2018). Also, the fish and seafood from the contaminated water can have serious health effects, especially to children and pregnant women. Besides, chemical fumes, smoke, and other industrial emission pollute the air. Moreover, the solid discharge from industry is huge, and most are nondegradable.

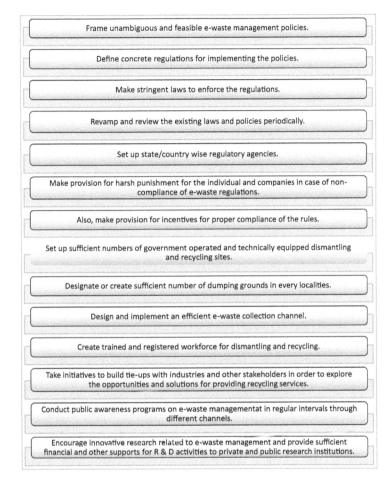

Frame unambiguous and feasible e-waste management policies.

Define concrete regulations for implementing the policies.

Make stringent laws to enforce the regulations.

Revamp and review the existing laws and policies periodically.

Set up state/country wise regulatory agencies.

Make provision for harsh punishment for the individual and companies in case of non-compliance of e-waste regulations.

Also, make provision for incentives for proper compliance of the rules.

Set up sufficient numbers of government operated and technically equipped dismantling and recycling sites.

Designate or create sufficient number of dumping grounds in every localities.

Design and implement an efficient e-waste collection channel.

Create trained and registered workforce for dismantling and recycling.

Take initiatives to build tie-ups with industries and other stakeholders in order to explore the opportunities and solutions for providing recycling services.

Conduct public awareness programs on e-waste managementat in regular intervals through different channels.

Encourage innovative research related to e-waste management and provide sufficient financial and other supports for R & D activities to private and public research institutions.

Figure 3.1 Government's responsibilities in e-waste management. (From ProKerala 2012.)

3.3 SUSTAINABLE COMPUTING

3.3.1 What Is Sustainable Computing?

Sustainable computing is a methodology that embraces a range of policies, procedures, programs, and attitudes for using any information technology. It is a holistic approach that includes power control and management as well as wastage management and education concerning the deployment of IT. The concept of sustainable computing considers the total ownership cost, environmental impact, and the

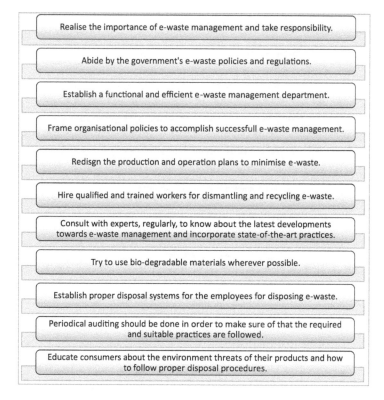

Figure 3.2 Role of industries and corporates in e-waste management.

benefits of the technology. Green computing, a notation of sustainable computing, has a goal of minimizing the use of hazardous materials, maximizing energy efficiency during the product's lifetime, and improving the recyclability of the product and the factory waste. Green computing is important for all classes of systems, ranging from handheld systems to large-scale data centres. In this chapter, we focus solely on the environmental aspect of sustainable computing.

3.3.2 Elements of Sustainable Computing

The following fours are identified as the core elements of sustainable computing, as shown in Figure 3.3:

Society: The people of society are one of the important key elements of sustainable computing. The ever-increasing demand for computers leads to manufacturing and purchase, putting a

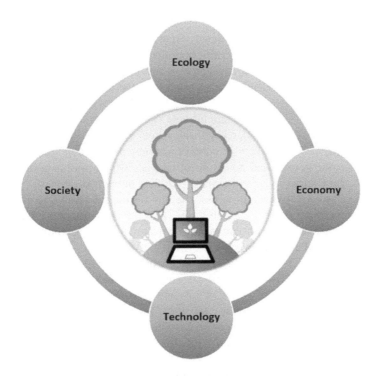

Figure 3.3 Elements of sustainable computing.

lot of negative effects on the environment. But it is the people of society whose careful selection of computing devices and judicious use and management may minimize the negative impact on the environment. People's wisdom and awareness could possibly reduce the carbon footprint and conserve energy.

Economy: The environment pays the price of a rising economy. Today's world economy is changing rapidly. These changing economies force the use of ICT hugely at all levels of business processing. Meeting the big market demand, industries are also bringing new technologies every other day. This fast-changing economy thus puts a negative impact on the environment. Stringent business policy, supporting the green computing model, would enable the reduction of the negative impact. Perhaps well-calculated and measured policies would be able to restrain the negative effect of the economy on the environment.

Ecology: Excessive use of computers over the last two decades has resulted in millions of tons of e-waste. This e-waste is continually damaging the environment by contaminating the soil and water. Besides, computer manufacturing has increased air and water pollution. Further, huge computer usages have a reason for enormous power consumption, resulting in more greenhouse gas emission. The negative impact on the environment is disrupting the ecological balance, thereby changing the marine and land life, vegetation, and climate. The water and air pollution profoundly impact land and water species, including endangered species. The toxicity in water or soil may pass through food and cause genetic and neurological changes which may pass on to generations in larger animals, including human beings.

Technology: As we progress, the environmental condition continues to deteriorate due to the adverse consequences of the industrial development on the environment. The technological advancement in every sector has made it worse due to more demands from people. In other words, technology is one of the culprits behind the ill environmental health. But considering the stage at which we are now, the only hope is also the advanced technologies towards sustainable developments. Sustainable technology and sustainable computing are important components of that.

Figure 3.4 shows the goals for sustainable technologies and sustainable development.

3.4 SUSTAINABLE COMPUTING FOR ORGANIZATIONS

Today, hardly any organization, be it small, medium, or large, can be found which has not adopted ICT. The emergence of cloud computing, AI, data analytics, business intelligence, and other cutting-edge technologies has escalated the embracing of ICT in every organizational sector. In addition to the externalities discussed in Section 3.2.3, there are other factors, especially for the organizational computing setup, which put more burden on the environment and human health. Some of them are mentioned in Figure 3.5.

In order to achieve sustainable computing goals, organizations are advised to follow the following essential suggestions for establishing and operating ICT:

Minimize: An organization can minimize ICT footprint without compromising performance or features in many ways:

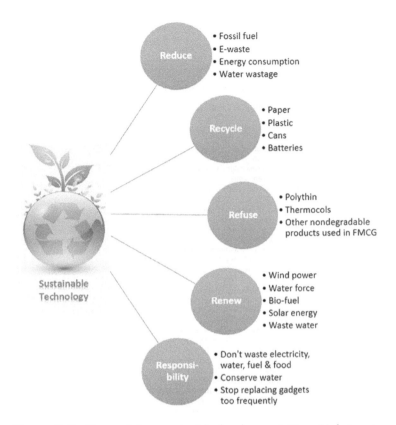

Figure 3.4 The goals for sustainable development. (From Maksimovic 2017.)

- **Only buy what you need:** Most often, organizations purchase faster and upgraded computers which they may not require for a job. For example, for simple word processing and web browsing task, buying a superfast computer with a high-end processor and huge RAM would be totally unnecessary. Aim to buy computers with minimal features just enough for performing the jobs, while allowing for any expected future growth.
- **Don't replace computers that work:** Many business organizations routinely replace their computers with new ones, even they are working fine. It is important that computers should be replaced only when it is absolutely necessary. This may reduce e-waste greatly.

Coolant	Heavy cooling is required to mitigate the heat generated from the computing systems.
	This consumes massive electricity.
	The coolant used in the air conditioners causes global warming and ozone layer depletion.
Batteries	Huge batteries are required for continuous power backup.
	Commonly used lead-acid batteries have adverse effects on human health and the environment.
	If not properly disposed of they may contaminate the soil and water.
Cleaning materials	Dusting and cleaning are important in organisational computing systems for efficient operation.
	Varieties of cleaning solution are available, and most of them are toxic as they contain bleach, ammonia, or chlorine.
	These toxic cleaning solutions have an adverse effect on human health.
Diesel fuel	Diesel fuel-based power generators are often used in case of power failure.
	These generators are used especially at the sites which experience recurring power failure, and batteries can not support for longer durations.
	Diesel fuel produces an enormous amount of CO_2 and other chemicals which causes global warming as well as affect human health.
Electronic waste	Electronic equipment have a finite lifespan.
	Most of the computer peripherals need to be replaced by 3-5 years which is increasing the amount of e-waste enormously.
	The e-wastes are not easily degradabel and are harmful to the environment if dumped on the open landfills.
Fire suppression	With electronic equipment there is always chances of fire due to short circuits, etc. Therfore fire suppression sytems are commonly employed.
	Various chemicals used in the fire system may be harmful to the environment such as ozone layer depletion and global warming.
	These chemicals are toxic and may find its way to underground water or to rivers, thus, contaminating the water resources.
Packaging	The packaging materials of the computing equipment purchased by the organisations add huge waste every year.
	Some materials like foams, thermocols, plastic bag, and plastic support accessories are nonbiodegradable and need proper recycling.
	Dumping these on the open area may harm the environment.
Office premises	Running air conditioners, heating equipment, and lights throughout the office for the entire day causes considerable electricity consumption and wastage.
	Daily office chores produce lots of paper, plastics, and packaging wastes.
	Floor cleaning, glass pane, computers, and carpets also produce chemical wastes.

Figure 3.5 Factors which affect the environment indirectly in an organizational computing setup. (From Kozlowicz 2015.)

- **Go small:** Organization should go for buying small computers like mini servers or thin PCs. Small, in this context, meaning they use less material to manufacture and are easy on the organization's limited resources.
- **Use energy-efficient computers:** Using computers and computing devices which are very energy efficient. Perhaps

using software which allows computers to reduce unnecessary power consumption is very important.

Offset: Choosing energy-efficient, ultra-small devices reduces pollution and conserves energy. The question arises on how to offset the remaining emission. Different solutions are available these days, choosing which we can offset the remaining emission. Some of the effective resolutions are tree plantation, turning to renewable energy, waste management, methane removal, carbon sinks, etc.

Recycle: Proper planning should be done before the disposing of scrap or old computers. Instead of throwing away the computers to fill the landfills, they should be refurbished and supplied to low-income people, communities, or organizations. Further, they can be disposed of to agencies which do the proper recycling of computer parts in many eco-friendly ways. Recycling computer components eliminates the dangerous impact of e-waste on the environment. At present, it is found that only 15–20% of all e-waste is recycled. Emphasis should be given to both, at the consumer level and at the bigger corporate level to increase the recycling percentage. Recycling of scrap or old computers can be done at the consumer and corporate levels, as explained below (Gajjar 2010).

- **Consumer recycling:** This type of recycling is initiated and carried by the consumers themselves. Consumers recycle old computers by donating to needy people or charitable organizations. Many consumers sell their old computers at a lower price to people who seek to buy cheap used computers. Auction firms like eBay also help consumers to sell their computers at a competitive price. This helps consumers in recycling computers for reuse instead of dumping them. Besides, companies offer a scheme to exchange old and used or defective computers for a new computer at a reduced price. These companies either service the old computers to sell them as refurbished products or recycle the scrap with the help of recycling agencies. Further, computer leasing programs help the consumer to get a computer as and when needed. This helps in increasing reuse rates and recycling the product again and again.

- **Corporate recycling:** Big business needs frequent computer replacements as stringent business policy. This causes discarding old computers at a large scale. Recycling these large numbers of computers is a big problem which every business faces. Mostly, the computer manufacturers or the third party carries out this recycling process. As a common practice, big businesses outsource the recycling process to the recycling agencies. It is the recycling companies which do the recycling of computers at the physical level. The recycling is carried out either by servicing the scrap computers by updating them to be sold as a refurbished product or by disassembling the components of the computers to be recycled on a part-by-part basis.

Judicious implementation of energy-saving methods: Proper planning and use of energy-saving components like the monitor, power supply system, processor, cooling system, and energy-conserving software help in minimizing energy consumption (Whitehead 2014). To minimize the power for cooling systems, the data centres may be designed to be natural air-cooled, or they might be shifted to the cooler places. Companies are now considering placing their servers undersea, which allows them to go reduce the electricity expenditure considerably.

Adopting effective e-waste treatment and disposal methods: Environmental pollution can be checked considerably by adopting proper treatment and disposal procedures to get rid of e-waste, instead of dumping on the open landfills or open burning. The goal of adopting proper waste treatment is to reduce the volume and toxicity of solid waste. Some of the fruitful techniques are (Leblanc, Waste Treatment and Disposal Methods 2018b):

- *Incineration:* In this method, e-waste is combusted in a controlled way, in the presence of oxygen. It benefits in a speedy decrease in the waste volume, waives transportation costs, and cuts greenhouse gas emissions.
- *Gasification and pyrolysis:* These two are organic decomposing methods where the e-waste is combusted with a very high temperature but with much less (gasification) or no (pyrolysis) oxygen. Gasification causes no air pollution at all, compared to pyrolysis.
- *Sanitary landfills:* In this method, the e-wastes are dumped in the specifically selected landfills where chances of pollution (soil and water) will be much less. For example, clay soil is resistant to toxic wastes; hence, for e-waste disposal, the clay soil rich landfills can be chosen. Similarly, the

location where the water level is very low can be chosen, which reduces the chance of water contamination. Though this method offers the least health and environmental risk, selecting or preparing this type of landfills is challenging and costly.

- *Controlled dumps:* This is similar to sanitary landfills but may not be that stringent in terms of choosing the land-fills. For example, gas management or regular cover may be absent, though it requires a well-planned capacity for dumping.
- *Bioreactor landfills:* This method uses superior microbio-logical processes to speed up waste decomposition in the landfills. The landfills are regularly fed with specific liq-uids which allow the landfills to sustain optimal moisture for microbial digestion.
- *Composting:* This is another organic decomposing method where small invertebrates and microorganisms are utilized for the controlled aerobic decomposition process such as static pile composting, vermin-composting, windrow com-posting and in-vessel composting.
- *Anaerobic digestion:* This method also uses biological processes to decompose organic materials. In this case, an oxygen and bacteria-free environment is created to decom-pose the waste material as compared to composting, which needs air to enable the growth of microbes.

3.5 COMPUTATIONAL MEASURES ADOPTED FOR SUSTAINABLE COMPUTING

The improvement of the energy efficiency of any given computer system without affecting the reliability factor is a major challenge to overcome in almost all the computing domains, be it a low-power embedded device or a large-scale server. Here, the key concern is the measures regarding how to reduce the power consumption where the fault tolerance technique needs computation and state redun-dancy, increasing the power consumption and a balanced trade-off between them. The trade-off can be managed by combining the techniques that comprise of both hardware as well as the software where it is impractical to concentrate over a single component or a level of the system on attaining adequate power consumption and reliability.

3.5.1 Low-Power Processors

Processors in computing devices consume a considerable amount of energy. This energy consumption varies linearly with the processor clock speed. To process, the increasing jobs demand clock speed is increased, resulting in high energy consumption. But not all the jobs require a powerful processor. Submitting the low-end jobs to the low-end processor will save significant energy. Even when the processor is idle, it consumes energy. In that case, also, a low-power processor will waste less power.

For sustainable computing, it is essential that processors consume low power. The development of low-power processors allows them to use much less battery power. Due to their low power consumption characteristics, they are suitable for mobile-based computing for a longer duration. It is an ongoing challenge to best fit the performance with power consumption. The chip designers are struggling to attain the most appropriate power–performance balance. The processor circuit is reduced, and the distance between the interfacing circuits is minimized to reduce energy consumption. Often, the memory and the input and output port are onboard fabricated to reduce the power consumption.

Manufacturers like Intel and AMD are putting forward new processor technologies where a single processor can do the job of multiple processors consuming an equal amount of energy. The multi-core processor technology (dual, quad, or octa-core processors) enhances the computing performance significantly by enabling parallel computing capability in a single processor package. The multi-core processor reflects as multiple processors working together with performance much higher than a single processor at lower clock speeds. The voltage consumption per core is less and, thus, typically consumes less power (Silicon Mechanics 2018).

3.5.2 Energy-Efficient Storage

Secondary storage devices (e.g., hard drive) are electro-mechanical devices which consume huge energy while accessing data from the magnetic disc. The magnetic plate sizes, the speed of data accession, read-write head movement, and data transfer are some of the factors which affect energy consumption. The development of a new storage device like Serial Attached SCSI (SAS) with the advantage of a 2.5-inch plate size model provides high performance with lower energy consumption in comparison to a traditional 3.5-inch model. Similarly, for less I/O-intensive applications, Serial ATA (SATA) provide high yield with less power consumption (Silicon Mechanics 2018).

3.5.3 Algorithmic Efficiency

The efficiency of an algorithm counts on the computational resources used by the algorithm. The increasingly complex algorithms need more space and time, which increases processor cycles consumption and thus the power. To attain maximum energy efficiency of an algorithm, its resource utilization needs to be minimized. For attaining sustainable computing, it is necessary that the algorithms used in computation jobs are energy-efficient or could be said to have the requirement of less hardware. For example, the time complexity of a hashing-based search is much less as compared to a linear search. This ensures hashing-based search uses less processor cycles and hence consumes less energy. In a study at Harvard, it was found that 7 grams of CO_2 are produced for an average Google search, which Google doubts and claim to be 0.2 grams. Irrespective of the claims, it is clear that an inefficient algorithm in terms of resource complexity could lead to the consumption of huge energy. Thus, for having sustainable computing, the energy efficiency of the algorithm should be considered as one critical parameter. Switching to an efficient algorithm would be a sustainable solution for energy-efficient computing.

3.5.4 Efficient Resource Allocation

Processing job requires various computational resources like processor, memory (internal and external), I/O devices, and other devices. For maximizing computational productivity, it demands an efficient strategy of resource allocation. The processes executing in parallel may often require resources which may be shared and held by other processes. A process holding a resource while not using it consumes a lot of resource energy. Efficient and intelligent resource allocation may help to solve problems like starvation and deadlock situation. The optimal resource allocation strategy ensures resources are properly allocated on a time and requirement basis to processes and are properly released, thus saving extra power consumption.

3.5.5 Energy-Efficient Routing

Routing is an optimization task of selecting an efficient and reliable network path for routing data packets. The various criteria for optimal path selection depend upon the distance between source and target, network bandwidth, shortest delay, and constraints like limited node power, restricted wireless link capacity, etc. It is seen as the number of hops increases, the network path selection, and transmission of data packets through different hops makes routing energy consuming. In sustainable computing, it is of utmost importance that energy-efficient routing protocols are used which uses fewer hops for delivering the packets.

3.5.6 Energy-Efficient Display

In a computer system, in comparison to the other components and peripherals, the display device (monitor) consumes the most energy. Even when the computer is idle, the display device continually keeps consuming energy. For sustainable computing, display devices should be energy-efficient. There are two ways seen for reducing energy consumption by display devices. One is integrating low-power consumption technology for display, and the other is efficient power management, which makes sure the display device hibernates when it is in an idle state. Earlier, the use of CRT technology consumed a lot of energy, but their replacements by LCD and subsequently, light-emitting diode (LED) technologies have reduced the power consumption considerably. Further, in comparison to LCD monitors, which typically use a cold-cathode fluorescent bulb to provide light for the display, the LED monitors use an array of LEDs. Thus, LED reduces the amount of electricity used for display; moreover, LEDs are mercury-free and nontoxic as compared to LCDs.

3.5.7 Operating System Support

The importance of designing an energy-efficient system has gained attention with the proliferation of portable and battery-operated devices, e.g., laptops, personal digital assistants (PDAs), mobile phones, etc. Various hardware solutions have been proposed as a method to minimize energy consumption where the energy efficiency in terms of software solution is comparatively unexplored yet. As software is the driving force behind given hardware, the decisions undertaken during software designs generally have a major impact on the overall system energy consumption. The operating system (OS) as system software manages the different components and resources of a computing device. From the research perspective, apart from the memory management in the OS, the remaining areas were never given focus in respect to energy efficiency. One of the functionalities of the OS is resource accession and scheduling them for use. Most of the time, when the computing system is idle or not in use, the OS continually accesses the different resources, and this makes the computer consume energy continually. In sustainable computing, the OS must be energy-efficient where the computing resources must be cleverly and efficiently used to avoid unnecessary energy consumption.

3.5.8 Efficient Power Management

Hardware components in a computer consume a huge amount of energy even when they are not in use (but kept on). For sustainable computing, it is absolutely necessary that the computer conserves energy. The criteria of power management for devices like CPU, GPU, and computer peripherals, e.g., monitor, printer, etc., is that they are able to manage the power efficiently by turning off or switching to a low-power state when non-active. Several efficient power management techniques available that make computers (Chedid and Yu 2002), HPC systems (Liu and Zhu 2010), data centres (Mittal 2014), and mobile devices (Goyal 2011) (Abdelmotalib and Wu 2012) (Shah, Chaudhary and Agrawal 2017) energy-efficient. For efficient power management, the computer hardware devices abide the Advanced Configuration and Power Interface (ACPI), an open standard, which allows the operating system to control and manage the device power directly, and hence when not required are set to off. CPU generally consumes high power with an increase in job processing and also causes heating, and thus extra power is required for cooling.

New power management programs called "undervolting" allows setting the CPU power manually. There are automatic undervolt programs available which automatically increase the CPU power on demand, like "SpeedStep" on Intel processors, "PowerNow!" or "Cool'n'Quiet" on AMD chips, LongHaul on VIA CPUs, and LongRun with Transmeta processors. Currently, most servers consume approximately 70% of the maximum power even when they are idle and consume 80% of their maximum when they are working at 20% of their peak utilization. In the server, power management is disabled to keep up the response time and performance. However, enabling the processor power management may allow the server to save energy consumption up to 50% in the idle state (Silicon Mechanics 2018). Highly efficient and properly designed power supplies reduce the power loss within a server, which results in significantly less energy consumption and heat generation while in operation.

3.6 SUSTAINABLE COMPUTING APPROACHES

3.6.1 Grid Computing

Grid computing, based on a distributed computing paradigm, allows connecting loosely coupled computers as one big virtual computer to accomplish huge computational tasks (Pramanik and Choudhury, 2018). In comparison to supercomputers, having multiple processors connected by high-speed bus, grid computing provides the environment for interconnecting the computers with atomic processing capability to serve one giant computational task. For future sustainable computing, grid computing is a suitable approach. The flexibility to adopt different computational devices supports reusing the idle heterogeneous devices for computing by the process called CPU cycle stealing. This is an excellent feature which makes use of existing unused active computing devices (mobile and computers) which otherwise in their idle state waste enormous processing cycles as well as energy. The grid, on the basis of the job requirement, scales up its computational power from the available connected devices. This makes sure that only the required number of computational devices are used without keeping the entire resources on hold. This, in comparison to other HPC facility (supercomputers), makes sure that the cost and energy are saved and would allow reusing the existing computing infrastructure at their best.

3.6.2 Cloud Computing

The concept of cloud computing may be stated as a shared pool of configurable computing resources along with quality services which can be rapidly provided on an on-demand basis with limited effort (Pramanik, Pal and Brahmachari, et al. 2018). The cloud computing services (hardware and software) can be scaled to any number of computer requests and thus eliminate the need for private data centres. For a business organization, the cost incurred for subscribing to a cloud service is comparatively much less than maintaining private data centres. The cloud technology, with its resource-sharing approach, has actually discouraged business enterprises opting for private data centres. Thus, reducing the number of data centres has significantly contributed to energy saving. Currently, many data centres have reduced energy consumption by embracing cloud technology. In this view, recently, Google has claimed that the use of cloud technology has reduced existing data centres' power consumption by 50%.

3.6.3 Serverless Computing

The concept of cloud technology has brought the serverless model, which allows dynamic handling and allocation of machine resources (hardware and services) on an on-demand basis. This eliminates the cost associated with the purchasing and maintenance of privately-owned servers. The cloud technology allows resource sharing, which makes optimum use of cloud resources in parallel for multiple purposes on a large scale. Serverless computing adds another layer of abstraction atop cloud infrastructure. It can be understood as the more exclusive version of platform as a service (PaaS) in cloud. In PaaS, a minimum set of resources has to be maintained at the client's end, whereas in serverless computing everything is deported to the remote server. The developers are freed from worrying about anything but their runnable code and functions which should be run and tested in the cloud server (Knorr 2016). As per the on-demand service provisioning principle of cloud, serverless computing is also able to scale up quickly by spawning new instances of resources as they are requested. Moreover, it also scales down quickly by shutting resources down when they are not required or if their use period is exhausted. This saves a lot of energy consumption. Serverless codes need not be run in any specific server; rather, they can run anywhere through the internet. This means the serverless applications can be deployed on the edge of the network that is close to the end users (Cloudflare 2019). This will not only reduce the latency but will also save a significant amount of energy by eliminating the need for unnecessary data transmission (Pramanik, Pal and Brahmachari, et al. 2018). Individual private servers consume huge energy. The ratio of job processing to energy consumption is disproportionate, with immense energy consumed while the server remains underused. Serverless computing saves energy consumption in running those servers. Therefore, this model is considered a key approach to sustainable computing.

3.6.4 Using Terminal Servers

The concept of terminal servers contributes to green computing. The use of a terminal server along with thin clients gives users the impression that the computation is carried in the very same terminal, while the actual computation takes place in the terminal server. The thin client uses up to 1/8th amount of energy in comparison to workstations and thus considerably reduces energy consumption. There has been an increase in the use of terminal servers and thin clients to create virtual labs. The terminal server software include Terminal Services (now Remote Desktop Services) for Windows platform and Linux Terminal Server Project (LTSP) for the Linux platform while Windows Remote Desktop and RealVNC can provide a thin client.

3.6.5 Virtualization

Provision of assigning workloads to the servers on a one-to-one basis may cause resource underutilization. This can be avoided by virtualization. Virtualization is the process of logically parting a server into multiple virtual servers or server instances sharing the same hardware resources and allows processing multiple applications or jobs on different virtual servers. Furthermore, virtualization supports the distribution of works among virtual server instance, ensuring the server resources are used effectively. Figure 3.6 shows how multiple workloads are consolidated into one physical server by virtualization. Dedicated application server consumes more resources than is justified by their workload. By virtualization, a physical server acts as multiple server instances, consuming less energy in comparison to separate dedicated servers. It is seen with this process of server consolidation up to 25% of power can be saved (Silicon Mechanics 2018). For performing, virtualization requires better hardware resources as a high-end processor, good memory and storage, ensuring performance effectiveness of virtual servers. The concept of virtualization

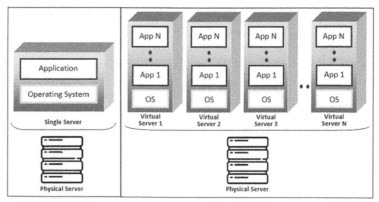

Figure 3.6 Traditional single application: Single server vs. multiple applications—single server using virtualization.

was first conceived by IBM in the 1960s for mainframe computers, and later on, the concept was implemented for x86 computers in 1990s. Many software companies have come up with software solutions for virtualization; this includes Linux container which effectively uses resources to reduce energy consumptions. Microprocessor manufacturers like Intel and AMD have incorporated virtualization enhancements to the x86 processor for supporting virtual computing.

3.7 SMARTPHONE CROWD COMPUTING AS A SOLUTION TOWARD SUSTAINABLE COMPUTING

The advancement of computing technology has miniaturized computers into the scale of few millimetres or centimetres. The new-age smartphone processors require less power and dissipate less heat. This brings to a new breed of evolutionary computing technology—smartphone computing. Evolution of smartphones has actually realized the miniaturization of computing devices with processing capability on par with a microcomputer. Even though the computation power of smartphone devices is less, the cumulative processing power of smartphones is quite big enough to resolve complex computational jobs. The philosophy of combining computation power of numerous distributed smartphones to escalate the computation power leads to SCC. SCC is established on the policy of sharing the CPU cycles of multiple smartphones in a distributed manner, voluntary or involuntary basis, to resolve high computation task (Pramanik, Pal and Pareek, et al. 2018). The easy availability of smartphones makes SCC flexible, which could be set up in an ad-hoc/on-demand basis. The distributed nature makes SCC highly scalable. Further, the computing paradigm does not require any upfront investment and offers better and enhanced computation in comparison to grid and supercomputing at comparably much less cost. The key enablers that have enabled achieving the SCC goal are mentioned in Figure 3.7.

Economically, SCC has the edge over other forms of HPC paradigms. But could it be environment-friendly? The small size of smartphones reduces negative externalities since they require less material in manufacturing and thus produce less manufacturing waste materials (Pramanik, Pal and Choudhury, 2019). Further, the contribution of e-waste of discarded phones also is very small in amount. The smartphone users' responsibilities toward e-waste management are mentioned in Figure 3.8. Moreover, running a smartphone requires less power as compared to computers, and also the availability of

Massive increase in the number of smartphone users	Smartphones have become indispensable nowadays.
	The number of smartphone users, worldwide, is estimated to reach 6 billion by 2020.
	To many people, smartphones have become the primary computing device.
	Increase popularity of crowd-sourced application as well as public intention to share resources.
Computationally powerful smartphones	Powerful CPUs: The development of ARM processors, the most popular processor architecture used in smartphones and supported by most of the major smartphone operating systems, has made them a serious contender in consideration for a range of scientific applications due to their high competence in floating point performance.
	Powerful GPUs: The modern smartphone GPUs are capable of delivering more than 800 GFLOPS.
	Powerful SoCs: SoC like Tegra X1 from NVIDIA can deliver 1 TFLOPS while the computing cores with clock frequencies 2.5 to 3 GHz have become common.

Figure 3.7 Key enablers of smartphone crowd computing.

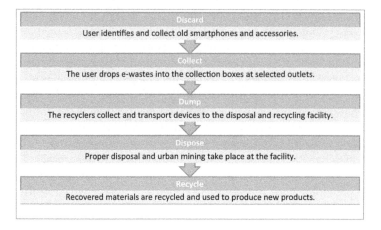

Figure 3.8 Smartphone users' responsibility for e-waste management. (From MCMC 2015.)

battery power eliminates the need for generator power sources. This reduces the carbon footprint considerably. Furthermore, smartphones dissipate much less heat in comparison to computers which exclude the use of a cooling system as used in traditional computing resources and thus cuts off the energy wastage in cooling. The biggest advantage in terms of environmental sustainability is that SCC does not require new upfront infrastructure in setting up the computing facility; the existing mobile devices of people can be very well used in computing. This liquidates the requirement and usage of new devices and reduces the burden of new products on the environment. The environmental advantages of SCC are summarized in Figure 3.9.

Even though SCC has theoretical and experimentally lucrative benefits, the commercial implementation has challenges which need attention. The SCC paradigm works by the participation of people by sharing their smartphones in computation jobs. Often, the sharing of smartphone devices is voluntary. But people are very reluctant to share their devices for third-party computations/applications due to data privacy concerns, data communication cost, and mobile battery usage. If the computation requirement is of social welfare cause, people might agree to share their devices. But if the computation job requirement has commercial viability, people would not agree to share their mobile devices without benefits in return. There is a lack of appropriate incentive model for this type of computing requirement system. The other challenges which require attention from the point of implementation are data communication and task farming. Since smartphone devices are mobile and all abide by different communication technology, availability of the mobile devices for constant computation is a big problem. Data communication in smartphones takes place through the internet service provider, Wi-Fi, and Bluetooth, and the reliability of these changes with vicinity and signal blockage. Since people move along with their mobile device, this causes problems in task distribution and computation task updates.

The implementation of SCC often follows a hierarchical master–slave model (Pramanik, Pal and Pareek, et al. 2018). Where a

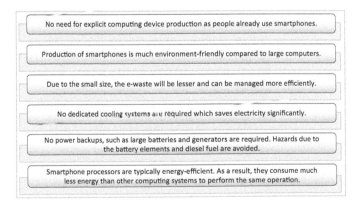

No need for explicit computing device production as people already use smartphones.

Production of smartphones is much environment-friendly compared to large computers.

Due to the small size, the e-waste will be lesser and can be managed more efficiently.

No dedicated cooling systems are required which saves electricity significantly.

No power backups, such as large batteries and generators are required. Hazards due to the battery elements and diesel fuel are avoided.

Smartphone processors are typically energy-efficient. As a result, they consume much less energy than other computing systems to perform the same operation.

Figure 3.9   Environmental advantages of smartphone crowd computing.

master node (mobile or stationary) distributes computational jobs to slave nodes. But, due to mobility, job reliability and QoS may be affected a lot of the resources join and leave the computational task group frequently. The mobility of the devices makes the choice of resource provider (smartphone) a tough decision-making challenge. Appropriate prediction and probability models help in selecting the smartphones in SCC. The other challenge is designing and developing middleware software which should take a computational task and disintegrate it into smaller tasks which are distributed into available smartphones, and then integrate all the results after the tasks are completed. But since smartphones are heterogeneous in terms of hardware and software, developing an application which allows uniformly joining smartphones in task groups and further splitting tasks and integrating the result is a big challenge (Pramanik, Pal and Pareek, et al. 2018).

Besides the other issues, limited battery capacity is probably the most bothering issue in implementing SCC. The quick battery drainage in the mobile devices discourages people in sharing their devices for SCC. The major challenges in SCC are summarised in Figure 3.10.

Motivating the crowd	People may be reluctant to offer their personal devices to be used by third party applications.
Adopting suitable incentive policy	To attract people to actively participate in SCC, suitable incentive policies need to be formulated according to the SCC application.
Security and privacy concerns	Since smartphones contains many sensitive user data there is always security and privacy threats in SCC.
Variable wireless network	The wireless services are notorious for their nonuniform transmission rate which might affect critical SCC applications.
Designing middleware	The SCC middleware and client application should support smartphones with diverse hardware and software specifications from various manufacturers.
Maintaining QoS	Maintaining QoS is really challenging in SCC, considering the factors such as device mobility, variable communication quality, diverseness in resources, etc.
Smartphones get heated	If the CPU is busy for a longer duration, the phone will be heated which may deter users from participating in SCC.
Limited memory	Smartphones typically have less memory than desktops/laptops which might affect some SCC applications requiring more memory
Battery power	This is the most detering factor in SCC. The limited power of smartphone's battery heavily impact the participants' willingness to lend their device.

Figure 3.10 Major challenges in smartphone crowd computing.

3.8 CONCLUSIONS

Global warming has become the most dreadful reality for the inhabitants of the Earth. This has resulted in erratic climate change, causing an increase in severe weather events from powerful storms to devastating floods and from deadly heatwaves to extreme snowfalls and notwithstanding the rising sea levels due to the melting of the polar ice plates. Industrial developments are the major reasons for deteriorating environmental conditions. Environmental effect is the most common negative externality for any industry. The damage is done through various forms, such as excessive energy consumption, carbon and greenhouse gas emission, heat generation, use of toxic materials in production, non-degradable waste generation, etc. To sustain the Earth's environment, we need to focus on sustainable developments. Sustainable computing is an important armament for that. In line with the data volume increase, the need for computing resource has increased tremendously. Along with the supercomputers, the traditional HPCs, recently cloud computing (data centres) have been popularized as a cheap and on-demand computing resource. But both of them have problems in terms of environmental externalities. Grid computing intends to use the existing resources (desktops) for catering to the needs of HPC. But desktops are losing popularity; in fact, same for laptops. While obsolete computers are a valuable source for secondary raw materials, they can also be a source of toxins and carcinogens, if not treated appropriately. Every country should have adequate e-waste management infrastructure with strict compliance to the e-waste management policies. Smartphones are gaining huge acceptance, and with the computing power they offer thanks to the power-packed hardware, they can be considered our new computer. Actually, they already have become our new computer for daily computing chores. If these abundantly available public-owned powerful smartphones are used as computing resources by forming a grid of smartphones, named as smartphone crowd computing, the generated computing power can well be compared to other HPC systems. The use of smartphones will lessen the externalities because the manufacturing process and device operation will be minimized significantly. Due to smaller size, less raw material will be used in production, which means less exposure to harmful elements and less pollution due to e-waste. If organizations can avoid buying computing resources, they can save a significant IT investment and operational cost. And fewer devices in production and operation means a direct benefit to the environment. It is challenging on the part of SCC to maximize energy efficiency to ensure maximum use of limited energy source available to smartphones while maintaining the required level of user satisfaction.

REFERENCES

Abdelmotalib, Ahmed, and Zhibo Wu. 2012. "Power Management Techniques in Smartphones Operating Systems." *International Journal of Computer Science Issues* 9 (3): 157–160.

Chedid, Wissam, and Chansu Yu. 2002. *Survey on Power Management Techniques for Energy Efficient Computer Systems.* Cleveland: Cleveland State University.

Climatenexus. 2018. "Top Climate Events of 2017." Accessed August 19, 2018. https://climatenexus.org/2017-top-climate-events/.

Cloudflare. 2019. *How are Serverless Computing and Platform-as-a-Service different?|PaaS vs. Serverless.* Accessed March 28, 2019. https://www.cloudflare.com/learning/serverless/glossary/serverless-vs-paas/.

Commoner, Barry. 1969. "Frail Reeds in a Harsh World." *Natural History* LXXVIII (2): 44–45.

Gajjar, Purvi. 2010. "Computers and the Environment." 20 August. Accessed August 17, 2018. https://www.mnn.com/green-tech/computers/stories/computers-and-the-environment.

Gelenbe, Erol, and Yves Caseau. 2015. "The Impact of Information Technology on Energy Consumption and Carbon Emissions." *Ubiquity* 2015 (June): 1–15.

Gillespie, Claire. 2018. "Negative Effects of Pollution." 11 June. Accessed August 26, 2018. https://sciencing.com/negative-effects-pollution-5268664.html.

Goyal, Kirtika. 2011. "Power Management in Mobile Devices by Various Protocols." *International Journal of Computer Science and Communication* 2 (2): 505–508.

Honda, Shunichi, Deepali Sinha Khetriwal, and Ruediger Kuehr. 2016. *Regional E-waste Monitor: East and Southeast Asia.* Bonn, Germany: United Nations University.

Jones, Nicola. 2018. "How to Stop Data Centres from Gobbling Up the World's Electricity." *Nature Research.* 12 September. Accessed February 24, 2019. https://www.nature.com/articles/d41586-018-06610-y.

Knorr, Eric. 2016. *What Serverless Computing Really Means.* 11 July. Accessed March 28, 2019. https://www.infoworld.com/article/3093508/what-serverless-computing-really-means.html.

Kozlowicz, Joe. 2015. "8 Ways Data Center Environmental Impact Goes Beyond Emissions." 11 November. Accessed August 18, 2018. https://www.greenhousedata.com/blog/data-center-environmental-impact-goes-beyond-emissions.

Leblanc, Rick. 2018a. "E-Waste Recycling Facts and Figures." 31
December. Accessed February 21, 2019. https://www.thebalanc-
esmb.com/e-waste-recycling-facts-and-figures-2878189.

Leblanc, Rick. 2018b. "Waste Treatment and Disposal Methods." 30
November. Accessed February 21, 2019. https://www.thebalanc-
esmb.com/waste-treatment-and-disposal-methods-2878113.

Liu, Yongpeng, and Hong Zhu. 2010. "A Survey of the Research on
Power Management Techniques for High Performance Systems."
Software-Practice & Experience 40 (11): 943–964.

Maksimovic, M. 2017. "Greening the Future: Green Internet of
Things (G-IoT) as a Key Technological Enabler of Sustainable
Development." In *Internet of Things and Big Data Analytics
Toward Next-Generation Intelligence*, 283–313, edited by Nilanjan
Dey, Aboul Ella Hassanien, Chintan Bhatt, Amira S. Ashour, and
Suresh Chandra Satapathy. Springer.

MCMC. 2015. "Mobile e-Waste: Old Phone, New Life." Accessed
February 25, 2019. https://mobileewaste.mcmc.gov.my/en-my/
about-mobile-e-waste.

Mittal, Sparsh. 2014. *Power Management Techniques for Data Centers:
A Survey.* Oak Ridge, TN: Oak Ridge National Laboratory.

Monroe, Rob. 2016. "Comment on Recent Record-Breaking CO2
Concentrations." 20 April. Accessed August 26, 2018. https://
scripps.ucsd.edu/programs/keelingcurve/2016/04/20/comment-on-
recent-record-breaking-co2-concentrations/#more-1406.

Monroe, Robert. 2008. "Potent Greenhouse Gas More Prevalent."
23 October. Accessed 31 July, 2018. https://ucsdnews.ucsd.edu/
archive/newsrel/science/10-08GreenhouseGas.asp.

Pramanik, Pijush Kanti Dutta, and Prasenjit Choudhury. 2018. "IoT Data
Processing: The Different Archetypes and their Security & Privacy
Assessments." In *Internet of Things (IoT) Security: Fundamentals,
Techniques and Applications*, edited by Sishir K. Shandilya, Soon Ae
Chun, Smita Shandilya and Edgar Weippl, 37–54. River Publishers.

Pramanik, Pijush Kanti Dutta, Bulbul Mukherjee, Saurabh Pal, Tanmoy
Pal, and Simar Preet Singh. 2019. "Green Smart Building:
Requisites, Architecture, Challenges, and Use Cases." In *Green
Building Management and Smart Automation*, edited by Arun
Solanki and Anand Nayyar. IGI Global.

Pramanik, Pijush Kanti Dutta, Prasenjit Choudhury, and Anindita Saha.
2017. "Economical Supercomputing thru Smartphone Crowd
Computing: An Assessment of Opportunities, Benefits, Deterrents, and
Applications from India's Perspective." *4th International Conference
on Advanced Computing and Communication Systems (ICACCS
−2017).* Coimbatore, India: IEEE. doi:10.1109/ICACCS.2017.8014613.

Pramanik, Pijush Kanti Dutta, Saurabh Pal, Aditya Brahmachari, and
Prasenjit Choudhury. 2018. "Processing IoT Data: From Cloud to
Fog. It's Time to be Down-to-Earth." In *Applications of Security,*

Mobile, Analytic and Cloud (SMAC) Technologies for Effective Information Processing and Management, edited by P. Karthikeyan and M. Thangavel, 124–148. IGI Global. doi: 10.4018/978-1-5225-4044-1.ch007.

Pramanik, Pijush Kanti Dutta, Bulbul Mukherjee, Saurabh Pal, Bijoy Kumar Upadhyaya, and Subhendu Dutta. 2019. "Ubiquitous Manufacturing in the age of Industry 4.0: A State-of-the-art Primer." In *A Roadmap to Industry 4.0: Smart Production, Sharp Business and Sustainable Development*, edited by Anand Nayyar and Akshi Kumar. Springer.

Pramanik, Pijush Kanti Dutta, Saurabh Pal, and Prasenjit Choudhury. 2019. "Green and Sustainable High-Performance Computing with Smartphone Crowd Computing: Benefits, Enablers, and Challenges." *Scalable Computing: Practice and Experience* 20 (2): 259–283. doi: 10.12694/scpe.v20i2.1517.

Pramanik, Pijush Kanti Dutta, Saurabh Pal, Gourav Pareek, Shubhendu Dutta, and Prasenjit Choudhury. 2018. "Crowd Computing: The Computing Revolution." In *Crowdsourcing and Knowledge Management in Contemporary Business Environments*, edited by Regina Lenart-Gansiniec, 166–198. IGI Global. doi: 10.4018/978-1-5225-4200-1.ch009.

ProKerala. 2012. "Responsibility of the Government on E-Waste Management." 21 July. Accessed February 26, 2019. https://www.prokerala.com/going-green/e-waste-management-and-role-of-government-and-indistries.htm.

Research and Markets. 2019. "Global E-waste Recycling & Reuse Services Market Size, Market Share, Application Analysis, Regional Outlook, Growth Trends, Key Players, Competitive Strategies and Forecasts, 2018 To 2026." January. Accessed February 18, 2019. https://www.researchandmarkets.com/research/lwvm28/ewaste_recycling?w=4.

Shah, Chirag, Sumit Chaudhary, and Priya Agrawal. 2017. "Performance Analysis of Efficient Power Management Controls in Android Device." *International Journal of Advanced Research in Computer and Communication Engineering* 6 (3): 83–89.

Silicon Mechanics. 2018. *Sustainable Computing at Silicon Mechanics*. Silicon Mechanics. Accessed February 21, 2019. https://www.siliconmechanics.com/i16642/sustainable-computing.php.

United Nations University Newsletter. 2004. "Study Tallies Environmental Cost of Computer Boom." Accessed February 18, 2019. http://archive.unu.edu/update/archive/issue31_5.htm.

Whitehead, Beth. 2014. "Measuring Environmental Impact Using Lifecycle Assessment." 16 June. Accessed August 18, 2018. http://www.datacenterdynamics.com/content-tracks/power-cooling/measuring-environmental-impact-using-lifecycle-assessment/87065.fullarticle.

WWF-Australia. 2018. *Causes of Global Warming*. WWF-Australia. Accessed August 28, 2018. https://www.wwf.org.au/what-we-do/climate/causes-of-global-warming.

4

CFD-BASED FLOW ANALYSIS AROUND THE MULTI-BODY SEGMENTS OPTIMIZED USING RIGID BODY FITTING METHOD FOR ROBOTIC FISH DESIGN

P. Raviraj, S. Raja Mohamed, and Adetan Oluwumi

CONTENTS

4.1 INTRODUCTION

Robotic fish design is an awe-inspiring study in the field of marine life engineering leading to the production of marine equipment capable of being smart and efficient in terms of shape, size, etc; modern-day application requires the system to be highly adaptive and energy-efficient. Here we have used CFD simulators such as SOLEIL and bio-hydrodynamics toolbox (BhT) to study the shape and size of real-time fish which can be incorporated into the design aspects of robotic fish. Materials used for caudal fin and their movement affecting water pressure and its jump are also tested using novel model to save energy under school of fish. Similarly, the number of rigid body segments coupled through relays to generate sinusoidal movement across the body or within the tail section is optimized using rigid body fitting method. Usage of Shape Memory Alloys (SMAs) leading to compact design and minimized energy consumption along with flexible materials used to design tail fin section to achieve maximum efficiency is also discussed to improve overall swimming performance of carangiform and ostraciform modes through relevant and possible key characteristics of fish.

The swimming model is realized after the concepts of improved Lighthill elongated body theory.

4.2 OPTIMIZATION OF MULTI-BODY SEGMENTS

Robotic fish have plenty of applications, especially the study of natural fish morphology and behavior as well as in environmental monitoring. They provide researchers with controllable reproduction to evaluate the behavior of real fish, or they can be used in the study of natural evolution and other biological hypotheses. Recent work, in which robotic fish interact with golden shiners, has shown that a tethered robot with a movable caudal fin can elicit schooling behavior from a natural fish in a water-flow tank [1, 2]. When the tail structure remained stationary, the live fish was not responding, supporting the hypothesis that a biomimetic robot can help in understanding fish behavior. As vindicated by the previous one, fish can act together with a realistic robot like a natural fish. With more and more refined designs, insight into fish actions can be taken to solve problems by observing biological fish in natural or a fixed lab atmosphere. At the same time, robotic fish were also used to observe underwater activities like oil spill detection, surveying, etc. As it appears similar to natural fish, mobile sensor can be placed to observe ecosystems without interference.

4.2.1 Fish Swimming

In this section, the existing robotic fish propulsion modes of oscillation and undulation have been discussed with various mathematical and simulation models and surveyed with its advantages and disadvantages.

4.2.1.1 Oscillatory Mode

Jindong Liu et al. initiated the study and design of a 3D robotic fish simulator to identify the suitable autonomous motion control algorithm [3, 4]. They analyzed it right from the software structure using object-oriented methodology and also discussed an interface which is interactive. They suggested three types of models, such as kinematics, joint kinematics, and hydrodynamics, to control the movement of fish. However, they had to develop an exclusive simulator which they purchased, CACIS. It was using sonar sensor model to find an optimal path by eliminating water wave noise affecting fish movement. It was suitable or supporting up-down swimming and also the autonomous navigation algorithm having limitations in terms of working inside a specific region only.

Pratap and Samrat analyzed fish motion inside water having oscillatory mode of swimming [5]. They dissected the hydrodynamics of robotic fish to navigate inside a 3D space with the help of tail and pectoral fins. From the work, it was a direct improvement on Jindong Liu et al. [6] with the models suggested in the same. Here, instead of simulation, a model robotic fish was constructed with additional tilt sensor to measure elevation, and trajectory was also noted. However, in this work they used only a mechanical pectoral fin designed using Autodesk3D. The main intention of this work was to design and develop a prototype model for oscillatory motion in a complete package using microcontroller (Atmega-128) and relays for increased robustness.

4.2.1.2 Undulatory Mode

Angus Webb et al. analyzed the limitations of Lighthill's Large Amplitude Elongated Body Theory (LAEBT) to model multilink-based robots used in undulation-based propulsion [7, 8]. It deals with elite swimming in 2D kinematic motion originating from reactive forces between the surfaces of the body and the volume of surrounding water for robots whose cross-sectional area is very smaller towards swimming direction compared to perpendicular direction of undulatory motion. Here, thrust and resistance forces were estimated for a prototype, and the experimental results show that EBT has the potential to provide detailed insight into hydrodynamics of robotic fish but with suitable refinement. This can be achieved by implementing a near perfect dynamics model for joints and their movement to consider even the wakes and vortices generated by segments of fish.

Omar Yaakob et al. developed a simple mathematical model for fish body undulations used to design and build innovative marine propulsion systems complementing the environment [9]. They took the case of catfish (*Clarias batrachus*), known for its undulatory motion in an aquarium, with the help of progressive scan monochrome camera to capture swimming sequences. Images taken from video recordings analyzed frame by frame with reference to local coordinate system. The heaving amplitudes of fin during undulation were obtained from each point marked on fish body, and a graph is drawn against amplitude and time to derive a mathematical model in the form of a polynomial equation having nine orders.

Grgur Tokic et al. proposed a muscular model having muscle contraction at certain time periods with relative kinematic and energetic related parameters to describe swimming [10]. They used an evolutionary algorithm with a multi-objective optimization towards sustained maximum speed and minimum energy consumption. The body shape primarily affects the hydrodynamics of swimming and also the muscle model too. They also found that Lighthill's EBT is unable to capture the long motion wavelengths and it does not care about the drag effects of the fish. However, with an appropriate Reynolds number, higher accuracy is achieved in their CFD simulation for viscous flow equations. They also classify the body shapes and size in to two categories with high speed and min energy consumption for varying Reynolds number to choose between.

4.2.1.3 Critical Parameters

George Lauder et al. studied the dynamics of locomotion and other effects of flexible plastic foils used to design caudal fin for a robotic fish [11]. They analyzed parameters such as length, stiffness, and kinematics. The study is made in two ways, one with heave and or pitch motion against a flapping prototype. They found certain nonlinear effects such as changing length and stiffness of foil and trace the trailing edge on self-propelled swimming speed and kinematics. The wake structure was also quantified using particle image velocimetry to describe the effects of heterocercal and homocercal tail shapes. They have come up with an interesting resonance phenomenon; the speed varies with length and even small changes have dramatic effects on speed with respect to stiffness of the foil.

Junzhi Yu et al. identified some parameters that may influence the propulsion of a robotic fish with multilinks connected through relays or mechanical joints [12]. They considered both theory and practical issues with respect to hydrodynamics. The number of joints that would make the fish propel and achieve maximum efficiency lies in the optimal link length ratio for a 4-linked robot fish prototype. They conducted experiments on forward swimming speed with and without optimization to prove the effectiveness. They also used a curve fitting algorithm to optimize the number of links and their respective length ratio to achieve max efficiency [13].

From the literature, it is observed that the existing oscillatory and undulatory mode of robotic fish swimming techniques have both advantages and disadvantages, but it mainly lacks, having the following limitations:

- Lighthill's EBT and Wu's waving plate theory for undulation and oscillation modes are not tested with parameters other than hydrodynamics.

- Only a selective list of critical parameters influence the flow around the body such as size, shape, and tampered areas towards the caudal fin section to control thrust based movement.
- A robust mathematical model which has to be tested in a simulator is always lacking to test hydrodynamics effects with changing critical parameters.
- Existing techniques are using procedures which are complex when the solution is available from nature itself.

To solve these issues, this research work aims to bring out an efficient swimming algorithm based on particle swarm optimization (PSO) and also to identify the procedure to design a prototype performing the same. Though there are millions of fish types existing, we have selected few specific natural fish models to do the experimentation to solve the issues as it has to be a bio-inspired solution, i.e., a nature-inspired computation.

4.2.2 Rigid Body Fitting Method (RBFM)

Fin design and fabrication is primarily about modelling fin structures originating from nature. Different types of swimming locomotion (anguilliform and carangiform) require specific mathematical models to exactly illustrate the motion dynamics. A ribbon-like fin with a string of actuators linked by a soft material has been shown to be capable of replicating the force of real fins. Further research gives insight into carangiform locomotion, in which forward thrust is mainly generated by the caudal fin. Recently, a mathematical model has been proposed to cover the different aspects of locomotion that pertain to bendable carangiform caudal fin [14]. To find a suitable method which can trade between complexity and computation with precision, we assume the body wave as a link of real objects having uniform force acting against them at any given point. Then there are series of straight lines hanging from the main axis toward the body wave, as shown in Figure 4.1, which tend to contract when it moves and also reaches a stable state and stops there. This can be considered as target position for which a mathematical model has to be developed [15, 16].

Based on the movement of dotted lines as shown in Figure 4.2, they are assumed to have a static head and moving tail, and the other one assumes all the joints to be totally free, leading to multiple degrees of freedom (DoF), which is very difficult to control. A rigid body α with erection and density f_x at the location x whose acceleration is noted as β as per Equation 4.3.

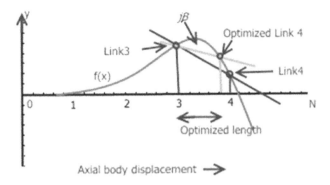

Figure 4.1 Optimization of link length ratio using joint method.

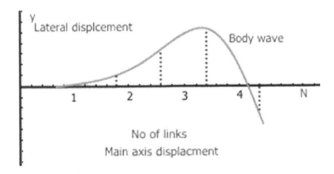

Figure 4.2 Rigid body fitting method for links.

Here head is assumed to be static; hence, the remaining parts only have movement, which can be described as follows: where x_h and x_t represent head and tail sections of the rigid body and j refers to moment of inertia followed by angular acceleration β

$$j\beta = \int_{x_h}^{x_\tau} f_x\left(x - x_\tau\right)\cos a\,dx \tag{4.1}$$

$$j = \frac{1}{3}ml^2 \tag{4.2}$$

$$\beta = \frac{3}{ml_x^2}\int_{x_h}^{x_\tau} f_x\left(x - x_\tau\right)dx \tag{4.3}$$

Overall, energy required to rotate the body with respect to erection force and angular acceleration can be described in a simple equation.

$$\frac{m}{2l_x} \int_{x_h}^{x_r} \left[(\alpha + \beta x)^2 + \beta^2 x^2 \tan^2 \alpha \right] dx \qquad (4.4)$$

Erection force and angular acceleration are computed separately using Equations 4.3 and 4.4. Shifting along the main axis will cause rotation of the previous segment. If the displacement is smaller than the length of the same, then angular displacement is proportional to angular acceleration. Change in $\Delta\alpha$ is shown below

$$\Delta a_e = \Delta y_j * \frac{\cos \alpha}{l_i} \qquad (4.5)$$

where lateral displacement y of the next segment and length of the previous segment is considered to calculate the angular movement for each individual rigid segment.

4.3 HYDRODYNAMICS OF FISH

The estimation of hydrodynamic forces posing on the robot fish is of high importance. It gives an essential anticipation of propulsive force. In addition, dynamic analysis of the surrounding fluid is done using CFD; plus, simulation of the fluid flow helps a lot in the process of designing the outer structure of the robot fish. It will even be possible to control the vortices with a perturbation flow control instrument. The CFD analysis objective is to simulate the flow passing through the tail during forward motion. It also evaluates the thrust performance of the tail using the 2D tail kinematics. In this analysis, the fluid was supposed to be single-phased and the flow to be distributed and incompressible. Here, a 2D robot fish is modelled using BhT by assuming flow around the robot fish body under two different cases.

In the first case, with robot fish being fixed and flow moving around, whereas in the second, the robot fish has real motion. It pushes water sideways by oscillating motion of its tail and the movement of its body. This mechanism is able to react quickly with high efficiency. Moreover, the robot fish has a turning mode, in which its body will rotate to the intended direction and start to wave. In this way, the radius of turning will decrease. The pressure distribution around the fish is shown in Figure. 4.3, the fish

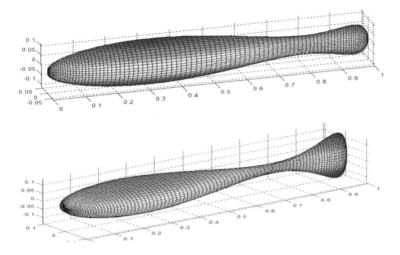

Figure 4.3   Optimization of shape and size using SOLEIL.

needing low energy expenditure for its propulsion. It shows that the tail produces vortices that pass to the downstream. These vortices can potentially enhance the thrust and produce low turbulence in the downstream. Another significant finding of the analysis is the smooth flow around the tail that causes high performance. CFD analysis can also provide hydrodynamic forces that are produced by the robot fish tail movement having mean value of the hydrodynamic coefficients produced by the robot fish in the steady analysis. There are two different force components produced by the tail waving in the unsteady analysis.

4.3.1 Fish Dynamics

Fish experience two major forces during underwater swim and they are listed as hydrostatic and hydrodynamic, where the former acts over fish even when it is not moving and the latter acts when the fish generates thrust to make movements in the aquatic environment. Hydrodynamic force is further described in two ways: one is reactive and the other is resistive with respect to fluid effects during propulsion, and also affect each other. Hence, the swimming behavior of fish has to be analyzed taking into account factors such as weight, buoyancy, reactive and resistive forces [17].

4.3.1.1 Fish Stability

While swimming, fish are exposed to dynamic forces inside water, as mentioned in the previous section. One such force that helps in understanding the balance of the fish is hydrostatic force. From the previous section, factors such as weight, buoyancy, and reactive and resistive forces are the mainstays behind balancing to achieve stability. Note that weight and buoyancy work in the contrary mode. Here weight W_f refers to the product of mass M of fish and gravity constant g. Buoyancy, according to Archimedes' law, is a product of volume, water density, and gravity constant.

$$W_f = M \cdot g \tag{4.6}$$

$$M = \rho_\alpha \cdot V \cdot g \tag{4.7}$$

$$B_f = \rho_w \cdot V \cdot g \tag{4.8}$$

Weight and buoyancy of fish together determine its position and stability depending on its perceptible weight, and if it is positive, the fish will sink or else float, and when the value is zero, current depth is maintained. This is the state that keeps the fish fairly buoyant. This naturally gifted character of animals living in ocean does not make them spend energy to pay off in achieving non-sink state. Perceptible weight determines the position of fish using the following term.

$$W_p = W_f - B_f \tag{4.9}$$

Positional stability of fish is based on the points at which M_c center of mass and B_c buoyancy lie. When they are equal and perpendicular to each other, then the posture of fish is in a stable manner. When the B_c is moved towards dorsal area compared to M_c, now fish get into a stable posture. Similarly, when B_c is moved towards the belly area compared to M_c, now fish get into an unstable posture. Based on the distance between M_c and B_c, stability is achieved at a specific angle, shown in Figure 4.4.

In order to perform moves involving maneuvers, M_c and B_c are not required in vertical positions as they do not allow changes in body position. Tuna fish normal cruising speed is around 2mph and when it's after squid and wants to whip it, then it can crank around the speed of 1/10 faster than its actual maneuvering speed. This is not just because of its fins but also due to hydrodynamics.

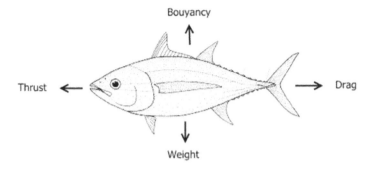

Figure 4.4 Orientation of weight and buoyancy on tuna fish.

4.3.1.2 Reactive Forces
Fish are able to swim in water by transferring the momentum into water and at the same time only a specific momentum is converted into thrust while the others are meant for a variety of movements. Propulsion of fish is based on two methods: one is oscillatory and the other is undulatory.

4.3.1.3 Oscillatory Propulsion
In general, under the oscillatory case, fish generate propulsive force by moving their body or fins in a wave-like pattern similar to a pendulum, which is done by the rowing or flapping actions done by pectoral fins.

In the case of propulsion, through the dragging mechanism which performs two actions in a single cycle which is divided into two states, one is propulsive and the second is recovery. During the propulsive state, fins are positioned at just about right angles to the water flow to increase acceleration and drag over its body. Then it repositions the fin to its previous state called recovery to generate the force again, and while doing so, to reduce the drag, it keeps the angle parallel to water flow. These two states are responsible for forward motion, and in detail only the first state is the ultimate factor behind thrust generation. Figure 4.5 illustrates the tract for both lift- and drag-based swimming styles according to pectoral fins [18].

Drag-based style swimming, another force that comes into the picture, is reaction happening due to acceleration and should be considered, as it affects surrounding fluid during acceleration and deceleration.

In lift-based swimming, fins operate like an aircraft's wing with aileron by placing the fins perpendicular to water flow to generate

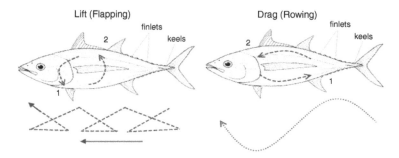

Figure 4.5 Lift- and drag-based swimming tract.

upward lift and parallel during downward movement. But the former is oriented towards downward and the latter remains constant by generating thrust during up and down states.

Fish swimming tracts are shown in Figure 4.6, illustrating the path of flapping or rowing fins with dotted arrows. In lift-based style, pectoral fins move up and down like a bird's wings. For example, tuna fish have drag-based mechanism and bird-wrasse have lift-based mechanism adapted for producing forward thrust. In the case of sea lions, propulsion force is generated by fore flippers in a downward

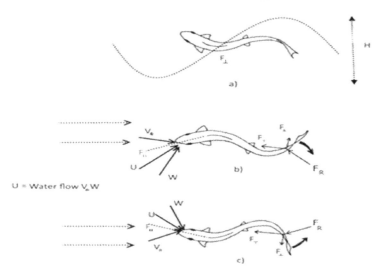

Figure 4.6 Undulatory motion of tuna fish with water flow U, fin orientation W, fish speed V, flow velocity V_0W, lift force $F_\perp$ and drag force F_T, oscillation amplitude H, angle of attack α.

sweeping action, and maneuver, the hind flippers are used. Zebra fish is the choice of study to analyze biomechanics, including school, balance, and neuromuscular transmission, known for their cruise and maneuver.

4.3.1.4 Undulatory Propulsion

Apart from the previously discussed oscillatory movement, the next most common type of producing propulsion force is by undulatory movement in which the entire body is involved in generating a wave faster than its swimming speed. Forces acting over tuna fish are shown in Figure 4.7. Fin orientation W and the fish velocity V_0 followed by flow speed is sum of these two, termed U. Water flow is affecting the fish body according to the fin direction and lift is generated when it's perpendicular to flow orientation at an angle α, which is called *angle of attack*.

In undulatory motion, swimming velocity of fish is lower than the frequency of body motion, then fish moves front way; if the velocity is low and wave frequency is high, then it's back way. In the case of lampreys, the entire body is involved in thrust generation [13]. Anyhow, forward motion is generated through reactive acceleration force and vortex shedding methods which are unique in nature [19]. The former is about the unsteady flow of liquid around the fish body, i.e., water to be displaced either for acceleration or deceleration by accelerating the fish itself, including the mass of fish and water. The latter is in terms of vortices generated by tail fin to displace water to

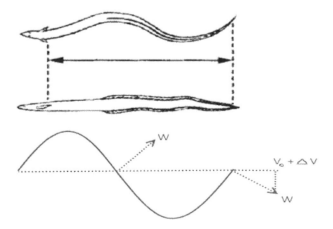

Figure 4.7 Undulatory motions of eel fish.

generate thrust. These two things together determine the swimming performance of fish.

In conjunction with the wave travelling across the body, reactive acceleration force F_R at an instance i is normal. It also has two more components acting parallel F_T and perpendicular $F_\perp$ to thrust direction, shown in Figure 4.8, which are lift and drag forces respectively. In a complete sequence of moves, perpendicular forces cancel each other to maintain the amplitude of the fish's lateral movement, and at the posterior end of fin, amplitude of wave widens by multiple waves based on the length of fish body. In case anguilliform, say, eel fish generate waves that are almost double with respect to body length at any point.

$$F_\perp = \sum_{i=1}^{n} F_{\perp,i} > 0 \qquad (4.10)$$

$$F_T = \sum_{i=1}^{n} F_{T,i} > 0 \qquad (4.11)$$

Alongside reactive acceleration force, vortices also generate undulatory motion similar to the characteristics of lift-based style of swimming by shedding them at the tip of fin as it is confined to posterior part of the body with evident force being generated mainly around the tail fin. When the fin is operating against water flow with an acute angle of attack, flow of water around the fin area is not going to symmetric, resulting differential velocity at either side of fin.

The differential velocity has two motions shaping at that end which are translational and circular in nature, shown in Figure 4.9. Difference in pressure, according to Bernoulli's principle, has inverse

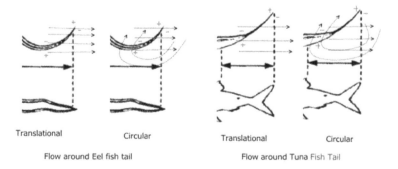

| Translational | Circular | Translational | Circular |

Flow around Eel fish tail   Flow around Tuna Fish Tail

Figure 4.8 Tuna and eel fish fin flow components.

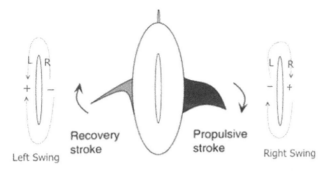

Figure 4.9 Vortex around tail tip of fish fin (posterior view).

proportional relationship with respect to flow velocity. When the fin is positioned at an angle α against the flow, then right and left leading and trailing edges have increased flow around them whereas the opposite edges have reduced flow. Now the flow will move toward the direction where pressure is high, where the fin moves in clockwise direction. Because of the differential pressure, circular movement of liquid happens. Vortex shedding due to the movement of fin changes its direction twice during swing at end of right and left side in one complete cycle. Vortices are not just generated on the sides but also at the tip of the tail fin.

To compensate for the differential pressure at either side of tail's tip, vortices are generated where the left- and right-side strokes complete one cycle. During the left-side stroke, flow pressure at the top of the fin is negative and the reverse when the fin moves in opposite direction, forming a circular effect over the tail-tip. Vortices shed at the tail combine together to produce forward thrust. But not all the vortices are contributing to propel the fish, wherein its efficiency is measured using a dimensionless parameter termed the Strouhal number describing ratio between wobbly state to inactive state, as illustrated in Figure 4.10.

$$S_n = 2\frac{fh}{\bar{x}} \qquad (4.12)$$

This parameter is applicable for fish that swim though their body and caudal fin, and its value hovers around 0.2 to 0.4, during which, vortices are able to produce maximum thrust, where f is tail beat frequency, h is amplitude of caudal fin, and $\bar{x}$ is mean velocity of fish. Vortices are generated irrespective of oscillation or undulation motion

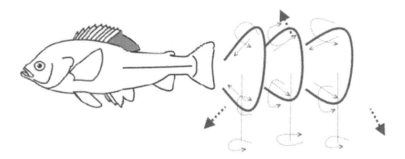

Figure 4.10   Vortex ring formation with direction.

using the same principle. Here, only caudal fins vortices are shown, but dorsal and anal fins could also be considered for optimization.

4.3.1.5 Efficiency of Reactive Force

Reactive or propulsive forces need to be compared according to the type of fish to analyze its functionality using the Froude efficiency η expressed as follows

$$\eta = \frac{\overline{F_c \dot{x}}}{E_{te}} \tag{4.13}$$

$$E_{te} = \overline{F_c \dot{x}} + \overline{F_c \dot{y}} \tag{4.14}$$

Conceptually, swimming efficiency can be measured with ratio between total energy and forward thrust with mean velocity. E_{te} is referred as total energy, F_{cx} denotes fish thrust, and $\bar{x}$ denotes mean velocity, F_{cy} denotes fish velocity and $\bar{y}$ length. At the same time, fish body and fin drive water backward in order to move forward. Thrust generated to swim is expressed as

$$T = u_w \left(dm_w / dt \right) \tag{4.15}$$

To calculate thrust u_w velocity of wake, m_w is volume of water displaced by fish and needs to be measured at a given instance. Now the resistive force will be having its hand in determining fish velocity. Fish thrust and mean velocity is multiplied to get the energy used to move. Optimal energy to move fish is calculated as follows

$$P_u = Tv_f = v_f u_w \left(dm_w / dt \right) \tag{4.16}$$

where v_f denotes velocity of fish and the P_k is the kinetic energy induced by water wakes again transferred back into it.

$$P_k = \frac{dE_k}{dt} = \frac{1}{2}v_w^2\left(dm_w/dt\right) \qquad (4.17)$$

Hence, the ultimate or total energy is calculated by

$$F_c\bar{x} = \left(v_f + \frac{1}{2}v_w\right)u_w\left(dm_w/dt\right) \qquad (4.18)$$

As we know the value of P_u and P_k, swimming efficiency can be obtained the other way around.

$$\eta = \frac{v_f}{v_f + \frac{1}{2}v_w} \qquad (4.19)$$

To improve the efficiency of fish swimming with help of thrust, the velocity of fish has to be high in comparison with water wakes or water resistive force. That means by reducing the water wake effects or turbulences, fish can be made to swim by making changes in size, shape of body, and fins for different modes. Tuna and bird-wrasse fish are efficient due to lift-based swimming mechanism, whereas eel fish deploy drag-based mechanisms by displacing more amounts of water in proportion to their fin size. An efficient swimming fish increases the speed of more amounts of water for acceleration and decreases the small amounts of water during deceleration.

It is obvious that undulatory motion has the advantage over its counterpart, i.e., oscillation motion, where more amounts of water are involved in thrust generation using body and fins. Even when we compare tuna and bird-wrasse swimming modes, the former has the outstanding efficiency with respect to the latter having oscillatory mode, as the tuna is able to displace huge amounts of water with its caudal fin peduncle section through undulatory motion. It is evident from the fin tract analysis, oscillatory motion coupled with drag-based mechanism is able to achieve only half the thrust using their fins, whereas lift-based mechanism is capable of using all the thrust forces, leading to high swimming speed.

According the reactive acceleration force, body friction and drag due to pressure difference is much less during vortex production. In vortex-based fish such as tuna, thrust is generated by the last part of the body by keeping the remaining section straight, but in the case of undulatory motion, the body is not straight at all at any instance, leading to an increase in both body and pressure drag. Hence, vortex shedding method needs less energy compared to reactive acceleration.

4.3.1.6 Resistive Forces

Fish swimming in an optimum mode is done by shifting energy into fluid by moving body and caudal fins where all of its energy is not converted to produce thrust because resistive forces are acting against them. So, fish swimming in an optimum mode is up to energy loss at an ignorable level due to resistive forces acting over fish body in the form of pressure and fluid viscosity. These drag forces or resistive force come into action based on the size and shape of fish body and its propulsion system and may be illuminated by dimensionless parameter R_e, called the Reynolds number. It specifies the ratio between viscous and inertial forces. Inertial or inactive forces are to be considered when the value of R_e is greater than 100, and if the value is 1, then viscous force holds the upper hand in acting against smoothness in swimming.

$$R_e = \frac{\rho l v}{\mu} \tag{4.20}$$

In the above equation, ρ, l, v represent fluid density, body length, and fish velocity with respect to fluid respectively. μ shows the wake form resistance of fluid due to fin movement. In lift-based swimming mechanism, the speed of flow velocity and angle of attack decides the forward thrust, whereas in drag-based system, the velocity of water being pushed backward during the first half of cycle is responsible for thrust and it's also equal to the differential speed between the fish as well actuators. Thrust increases when the difference of these two factors increases. This can be realized when the fish is in an idle state; as it starts swimming, the difference becomes very low and cannot be increased beyond a limit. Hence, this can be deployed when there is a need for instant acceleration or to perform sudden maneuver. As stated earlier, lift-based mechanism depends on flow velocity. In the initial stage, the speed of fish with respect to water flow is nil, but during swimming, fins are placed across the flowing water to generate propulsive energy for cruising. Hence, it is more suited to long distance swimming.

The following points are to be considered:

- Lift-based swimming style is very efficient compared to drag based.
- Undulatory modes are efficient compared to oscillatory.
- Cruising or periodic motion need lift-based undulatory motion.
- Drag-based swimming is suitable for instant acceleration.

4.3.2 Optimization Factors

Optimal propulsion can be achieved by identifying the parameters that are affecting swimming performance. There are two forces a fish has to deal with, and they are hydrostatic and hydrodynamic. First one acts even when the fish is not swimming or moving inside water. Second one is propulsive and resistive forces that act upon during locomotion or movement.

4.3.2.1 Weight and Buoyancy

So, the following elements such as weight, buoyancy, propulsive, and resistive forces are investigated in order to achieve optimum swimming. It is mainly decided by the stability defined using Archimedes' law.

4.3.2.2 Resistive Forces

The fish has to transfer its momentum to the fluid for motion, but at the same time everything is not converted into thrust. That means it will have certain forces lost due to resistance, and energy loss must be compensated to improve swimming efficiency. Resistance is mainly created by fluid viscosity, i.e., skin friction and pressure gradient, i.e., pressure drag along the body of fish. It can be analyzed using the Reynolds number, which is a dimensionless parameter indicating the relative importance of inertial force to viscous force. In most of the cases, having more thrust have large Reynolds number, whereas viscous effect is having ignorable amount of drag.

4.3.2.3 Propulsive Forces

As mentioned in Section 4.1, there are two types of modes: oscillatory and undulatory. In oscillatory mode, its body will create pendulum-like movement in a stable manner, and it includes two stokes, i.e., propulsive stroke, where the fin moves in the backward direction perpendicular to flow, and recovery stroke, where it moves in the forward direction parallel to flow. Hence, during propulsive stroke, acceleration and drag is increased, and during recovery stroke, drag is reduced to low. In lift-based swimming, fin is parallel to flow and uses a small amount of angle of attack. Here the fins are actually flapping like the wings of a bird, similar to aerodynamic lifting of flying object. The same can be seen in the form vortices during each stroke.

Undulatory mode is the one that is widely adapted by many fish as it generates a wave to propel using their body and fins faster than their swimming speed. Interestingly, if the speed of the travelling wave is higher, it moves in the forward direction, and if it decreases, then it moves in the backward direction. Vortex shed by the wave-like movement is measured by the Strouhal number, which, again, ia a dimensionless parameter representing the ratio of unsteady to inertial forces. Finally, to calculate the efficiency of swimming, propulsive forces are to be compared with respect to unique swimming characteristics of fish, using Froude efficiency. It is being calculated against the amount of work done to push forward and the total work done for locomotion along with other induced forces.

4.4 MATHEMATICAL MODEL

4.4.1 Improved Lighthill's Large Amplitude Elongated Body Theory (LAEBT)

With the help of rigid body dynamics, caudal fin motion can be approximated by dividing the fin into a number of discrete segments coupled by a spring and damping system. Yet the fluidic movement of a fin during locomotion is tough to model in simulation and difficult to replicate on a physical robot too [20]. It was proposed to illustrate patterns of a real fish's motion as if the entire body is flexible, and the movement of robotic fish at any point can be approximated using equations that result in the thrust and movement of the same [21, 22].

$$Y = (c1(x - x0) + c2(x - x0)2)\sin(kx + 2\pi ft) \qquad (4.21)$$

Basically, three different fin shapes have been considered in our testing. To calculate the forces produced by various fin shapes based on improved Lighthill's theory [23, 24]. In this model, robotic fish body is divided into equal-sized segments and the caudal fin converging towards the end to get the hydrodynamic forces evaluated independently for each segment along with additional force acting at the tip. The fin segments in the mathematical model are assumed to be connected through a series of relays forming a flexible fin structure, as shown in Figure 4.11.

4.4.2 Viscous Vortex Domain (VVD)

For computation of the flow around the bodies of variable shape, it is convenient to use meshless methods. We used VVD method. This method has been developed for numerically solving the 2D Navier–Stokes equations in Lagrangian coordinates. Among the well-known numerical schemes for the fluid flow simulation, the diffusion velocity method is closest to ours. The two methods differ by formulas that are used for calculating the diffusion velocity. In the VVD method they are well-founded and include no arbitrary parameters. The VVD method allows for a more accurate simulation of the evolution of vortices than one does it in especially near surfaces. It properly describes the boundary layers and allows calculation of the friction force at the body's surfaces. The equations describing the motion of the body can be incorporated into the system of hydrodynamic equations, so there is no limitation on the value of inertial characteristics of the body. In particular, we can operate with the case of zero body mass.

4.4.3 Bio-Hydrodynamic Simulation System

An environment to face the unique challenges with respect to modelling the fluid dynamics of an aquatic environment, BhT and SOLEIL were used in conjunction with the above mathematical model to predict the hydrodynamic forces acting on a caudal fin [25]. In turn, it avoids complex and time-consuming computational fluid dynamics calculations. Subsequent reduction in computation time is advantageous,

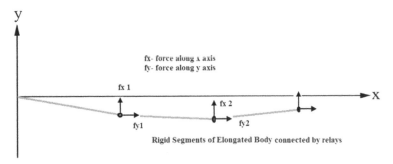

Figure 4.11 Forces acting over segments.

especially for evolutionary experiments in which a number of solutions are to be tested through simulation. The mathematical model restricts motion to a two-dimensional plane and assumes floating tendency without any outside forces.

This term was first used by biologists and zoologists while studying animal locomotion in fluid (fish, aquatic mammals, even in cases of birds where aerodynamics is involved). The investigations to realize the locomotion of aquatic animals have offered many things to scientific publications and the researching society. Such strong interest has made people observe aquatic mammals and fish in finding their evolved swimming capabilities far superior to what has been achieved by naval technology. A complete knowledge of biomechanics of swimming robots allows us to improve the efficiency, maneuverability, and stealth of underwater vehicles [26].

During the last five decades, various numerical models were introduced through which qualitative study of swimming propulsion was done, also combining previously developed quantitative theories. BhT has a collection of M-Files for design description and performs simulation cum analysis of articulated bodies' motions in fluid based on Euler–Lagrangian formalism. Apart from that, it can also carry out any type of numeric experiments related to the motion of solids in fluids (fluid–structure interaction system simulation). This is a tool for designing, simulating, and the analyzing the animal motions in fluids modelled as systems of articulated rigid solids by incorporating the rigid body fitting method based on Equations 4.3 to 4.7. It performs any kind of numerical simulation involving 2D motion of solids in aquatic environment without vortices, illustrated in Figure 4.12 and 4.13 with velocity in blue line and angular acceleration in red line at each instance.

Thrust generated by three-link mechanism is shown in Figure 4.13 at discrete time intervals. Energy is another factor affecting the performance of rigid body segments coupled by relays having lateral and longitudinal displacement. BhT analyzes the energy distribution across the hinge as well as the fluid surrounding fish body. Velocity and angular acceleration can be tested before performing continuous simulation.

4.5 ENERGY SAVING UNDER FISH SCHOOL

In the case of existing studies, the energy gathered from fish schools and spent was mainly in relation to specific patterns of swimming.

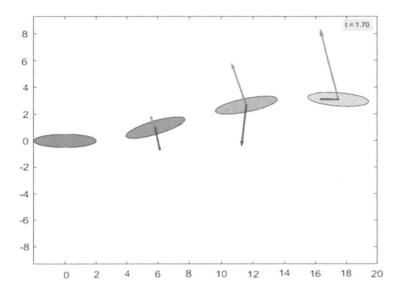

Figure 4.12 Velocity and angular acceleration over link mechanism.

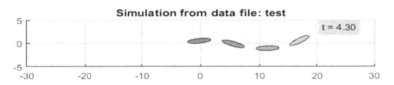

Figure 4.13 Link rigid segments' forward movement.

Among the formation hypotheses, a widespread example is the diamond pattern proposed by Weihs. But in the recent past, based on
computational models, it has been predicted that group configurations including diamond, rectangular, phalanx, and line are all hydrodynamically offering advantage in yielding energy. Advanced studies
on the real fish school confirmed energy savings irrespective of individuals' spatial positions. Whether the location is a crucial factor for
energy expenditure when fish are swimming in groups is still divi-
sive. At the same time, other factors related to energy consumption
are mostly unexplored.

Here, we consider a group of two fish-like robots swimming in a
laminar flow. The high fidelity of our robotic fish lies in its body shape,
bio-inspired locomotion, and Reverse Karman Vortices (RKV) shedding in similar form on either side by the caudal fin. The flow first

encounters the rigid head and then the flexible body. Thus, a realistic body shape is critical. The locomotion should be similar to the real fish to generate a similar flow field. Furthermore, the energy transfer between fish in a group is inclined toward vortices near the caudal fin; generating similar wakes is significant [27].

In the above investigation, we check and evaluate the power consumed by two robot flapping fish fixed in a flow tunnel at different relative positions and phase differences (PDs) in swinging its fin. To perform undulated movement in the fish body inside the field, the robot will consume power to overcome the resistive force of water acting upon. When they condense into a group state, interacting with water may lead to changes of energy cost to keep them doing the same movement across the body. Through chains of trials, we find that the trailing fish will profit from saving energy when swimming in some conditions, and when they group, it swims in the similar spatial arrays of the real fish, leading to cost of energy dependent on phase difference alone.

4.5.1 Power Consumption Method

Usually, the electrical energy fed into the robotic fish will be changed into mechanical energy and other energy forms such as heat. For the swimming robot, the energy that is useful is the mechanical one, which overcomes the reactive forces of the fluid interacting with its body. We calculate this part of energy consumption by subtracting the energy consumption when the fish is swimming in ideal conditions from the energy consumption when it swims inside fluid. Thus, the power consumed by fish swimming alone in fluid is evaluated as Pwa–Pa, where Pwa indicates the total power input when the fish swims in water alone, and Pa represents the total power consumption while the fish swims in ideal water. Likewise, we calculate the power consumption for a robotic fish swimming in group by Pws–Pa, where Pws is the total power consumption when the fish swims in water in school. To weigh against the power consumption between fish swimming alone and in groups, a power coefficient number η is defined as follows,

$$\eta = \left(P_{wa} - P_a\right) - \left(P_{ws} - P_a\right) P_{wa} - P_a = P_{wa} - P_{ws} P_{wa} - P_a \quad (4.22)$$

A positive value of η specifies power reduction when fish swimming in groups. Whereas, a negative value of η means fish in group will use more energy for simple calculation purpose. Notably, all the values are time-averaged as the power consumption varies in one oscillation period.

For each relative position and phase difference between robotic fish, the tests include power acquisitions of robotic fish swimming in air, in water alone, and in a school. Uncertainties during the test quantities are defined as the standard error of the mean $\sigma = \sigma/\sqrt{N}$, for each situation consisting of N =5 measurements. And σ is the sample standard deviation.

4.5.2 Reduced Swimming Cost with Phase Difference

Initially, a single fish swims and then we introduce a second robotic fish into the flow with a fixed SS of 0.4 body length and a series of lateral space. The power coefficient is calculated at each spatial lattice as well as phase difference for 10 trials. The estimated error is calculated to find the mean difference. The variation of power coefficient as a function of phase difference is quite similar to a sine curve and is little related to spatial factors. Fish school swimming with PD around 0.4 π will consume more energy in schools, while around 1.2 π schooling will lead to energy saving. Our data show that school fish energy saving is more related to phase differences than spatial lattice.

To prove the hypothesis, we compare the power variation by fixing the phase difference 0.4π. In all the areas, fish swimming with phase difference of 0.4π costs more energy while phase difference of 1.2π consumes less energy, indicating that the power consumption is more related to the phase difference than the spatial lattices.

To further study how the spatial and temporal factors affect the power consumption of group robotic fish, we carry out all the situations within the ranges, totaling more than two thousand trials. The power coefficient as a function of streamwise space (SS) and phase difference with four different lateral spaces. In contrast to swimming alone, the trailing fish may enjoy energy saving or suffer extra energy cost when swimming in different arrays and PDs. For almost all the locations around the leader, the follower will have the benefit of saving energy when swimming with a phase difference ranging of 0.8π–1.4π. The larger the SS, the less energy the follower saves. However, we find that, at larger SS, the trailing fish need larger PD to get a maximum power reduction. This indicates that the spatial array also plays a role in the power cost of the trailing fish but with less impact than the PD. Among all the trails we did here, the maximum power reduction for the follower is 6.9%, and the power increase is 5.6%.

When the direction of the induced vortex dipole is the same as that of the flapping tail, the follower will benefit from energy saving. On the contrary, when the flapping direction is opposite to the direction of the induced vortex dipole, the follower will consume more energy. Since PD describes the body wave of the follower leads or lags that of the leader, the relationship between the flapping direction and vortex-dipole direction is also determined by PD. When the schooling fish swim near (around 0.5 1BL), the energy consumption of the follower is greatly controlled by PD instead of space array. For all the PDs, PD around 1.2π leads to maximum energy saving for the follower swimming in school, and PD around 0.4π makes the follower consume more energy.

Further, one can definitely find that, with a phase difference of 1.2π, the follower swims in the same direction of the flow field induced by the vortex dipole, thereby saving energy. The follower with a phase difference of 0.4π swims in the opposite direction, and thus it costs more energy. As the flow field induced by the vortex dipole is determined by the leader's flapping tail, the energy cost of the trailing fish essentially depends on the PD.

4.5.3 Shape Memory Alloys for Reduced Energy Consumption

An SMA is capable of retaining its initially determined shape while encountering deformation through thermal effect. It is a real finding of the century involving nickel and titanium composition when it comes to energy consumption, as it consumes much less energy in activating the segmented body of robotic fish. It does not drain too much energy out of the battery of any other power source due to the nature of its flexible materials' nature. It actually bends and reverts to its original structure when power is being passed and cut off. Still, there is a limitation for SMA which is the latency in terms of cooling its wire after generating heating power. Research is ongoing in cooling the system quickly to overcome the recovery process in time. William et al. [28] have developed a robotic fish using SMA-based artificial muscles to perform fish-like swimming, including accurate movements and steady-swimming similar ray-finned fishes.

They introduced a PIC microcontroller-based mechanism to find the best suited vibration frequency generating the body and tail fin wave based on maneuvering and swimming. Finding the minimum amount of current passing through SMA structure for actuation, and the same being the susceptible to sensors, helps in getting the system even more inclined to the environment. Still, there is loss of energy in the form of heat, but when compared to the traditional electromagnetic relays, it stands out very high.

4.6 SIMULATION TOOLS

4.6.1 Bio-Hydrodynamics Toolbox

To perform simulation, a platform is required that can bring the real-time environment to some extent. Here we have used two MATLAB®-based packages that are called BhT and SOLEIL; 2D and 3D simulation functionalities, including motion analysis of fish inside fluids and even motion and path planning with optimal, can also simulated or investigated [29]. It has collection of MATLAB files, as shown in Figure 4.14, that can be used to simulate the structure of fish and its movement inside inviscid and incompressible fluid in two-dimensional solid segments. Body segments are hydrodynamically coupled with buoyancy, and collision of segments are simulated using time function by Munnier [30]. Here, in our case, vortex shedding and fluid structure interactions are described according to the LAEBT model.

Locomotion of fish is realized in a series of solid objects passing through fluid by leaving the inner mechanism out of equation by considering only the outer body and its shape to move forward and maneuver, which is shown in Figure 4.15. It has its own data file compiled with boundary check, and then trajectory is calculated in a matrix form along with kinematics for movement defined as a function of time. BhT uses Nystrom's method to compute fluid potential in shorter time by deploying NBVP. It also computes the energy distribution across all the joints for dimensions mentioned.

BhT allows the swimming object to be defined in the form articulated segments, having boundary with its control and kinematics generated by respective functions checked internally to calculate the trajectory or path to be fed for simulation and even computing the energy spent by joints or links during locomotion.

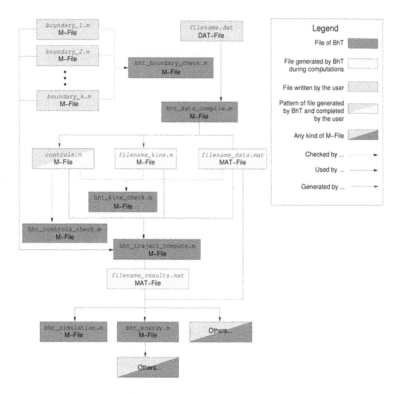

Figure 4.14   Features of bio-hydrodynamics toolbox.

Figure 4.15   Articulated polygon segments of fish body using BhT.

4.6.2 SOLEIL

SOLEIL is the platform using linear integral equations realizing the Newton–Euler formalism used for optimal size and shape exclusive for oscillatory and undulatory motion where the body segments are assumed to elliptical slices. BhT is an exclusive tool for undulatory motion to simulate multi-body segments and fluid interactions with respect to its boundary conditions.

SOLEIL has a collection of MATLAB functions developed to simulate fish swimming in fluid free of vortices (Chambrion, 2012). Generally, it swims alone in the fluid without any boundary. It performs simulation in 3D mode, as shown in Figure 4.16, where the hydrodynamic forces are solved using integral equations without defining mesh structure. Apart from that, motion planning, optimal shape, and swimming methods can be analyzed. SOLEIL does support only vortex-free swimming without boundary descriptions, but we have made modifications in such a way that vortex shedding can be modelled with the help of Strouhal number for optimized swimming. It uses a beam model by slicing the body orthogonally in an elliptical form centered on the spinal bone.

There are two functions providing the values for the major and minor axis of elliptical cross-section across the fish body sliced at each moment, describing the geometry of fish main axis. It calculates the density of fish with respect to fluid density to find the relative values.

Position and orientation of the fish is represented using a vector by generating a matrix with rotated elements. Internal frame of reference is mentioned along with the fish surface. Hydrodynamic forces are solved using seven Laplace equations referring to elementary Kirchhoff's potentials.

It is a basic ordinary differential equation solver paired to integral components. When considering the formation of surface mesh

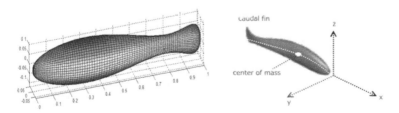

Figure 4.16 (a) Fish shape description (b) Swimming without vortices using SOLEIL.

defined in a triangular form, half of the mesh value becomes the step value. Overall deviation from the center of mass is around 0.25%, and the same goes below 1% with rough discretization.

4.7 RESULTS AND DISCUSSION

The characteristic parameters in the simplified propulsive model of bio-mimetic robot fish were optimized based on hydrodynamic properties [3]. The optimal link-length ratio was numerically calculated by an improved constrained cyclic variable method, and applied in BhT simulation of the three-linked robot fish.

Here we have proposed an evolutionary design method for robotic fish caudal fins and demonstrated the same. First, an adequate simulation environment, i.e., BhT and SOLEIL, were developed with modifications in which different fin configurations were to be tested. The simulation environment had a rigid body dynamics engine with a mathematical model of a flexible caudal fin's hydrodynamics exclusively for aquatic environment. To test the environment, first, hill-climber algorithm was used with a fixed fin shape and control pattern, to find fitness landscape for fin stiffness against velocity. The above results were compared to data generated from the model, which helped us in confirming the simulation and the mathematical model with comparable dynamics, despite the absolute values differing.

The simulated and physical results discussed here show the effectiveness of an evolutionary-based approach with dimensionality. Still, the work is not over, as we can focus on improving the overall design process. Here, assumptions central to the hydrodynamic model can be ignored; say, the body will no longer be considered as static and the fins without mass followed by gradually relaxing the constraints placed on evolution. Ultimately, several aspects of the robotic fish can be evolved in a process which can be generalized to any non-linear robotic environment.

4.7.1 Shifting Pressure around the Body

The undulatory or oscillatory motion of a flexible hydrofoil in a fluid may determine a thrust force. We present a method to calculate the thrust force by solving an integral equation which appears in the hydrodynamics of non-viscous fluids. This approach is a simplified one because one has to take also into account the viscous drag and other hydrodynamical effects. For a complete study of the motion of a robot fish one has also to take into account the motion control, the autonomous navigation and other aspects of the interaction between the robot fish and the water.

4.7.2 Rigid Body Dynamics

The flexible part of fish consists of many rotating hinge joints. It can be modelled as a planar of links along the main axis [22]. There are three links, i.e., (l1 to l4), between the joints. l_j (j=1, 2, ... , N) is the link length ratio and N is the joint number. Also, two end-point coordinate pairs of each link are determined (x_{j-1}, y_{j-1}), (x_j, y_j) and the joint angle between l_{j-1} and l_j is #j [29]. Primarily, the amplitude coefficients, i.e., (c1, c2, k), are determined, and swimming functions of the discrete travelling wave are founded respectively. The joint angle of the *j*th link can be computed by fitting them based on the body wave of *i*th instance and the joint angles (θ_1, θ_2, θ_3) are set in an array [29] for BhT simulation.

These operations performed by the equations describe the movement of rigid segments connected by relays. Swimming functions of the discrete travelling wave are used to determine the motion of the robotic fish, as shown in Figure 4.17.

Two dimensional matrices are obtained for each joint angle. θ_{ij} is used to control the movement of the fish. Here, various link length ratios. as mentioned in Table 4.1, are used for analytic fitting solution, having three joints or links, as shown in Figure 4.18.

Initializing the parameters of links segments are listed in Table 4.1 and the distance of servo links with respect to head section is shown in Table 4.2. Rigid body simulation method avoids the displacement parameter calculation beyond second order derivatives and produces comparatively better link length ratio even when *i*th link is far away

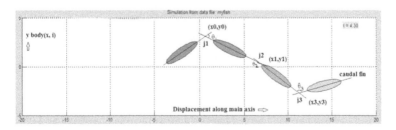

Figure 4.17 Body wave curve fitting based on three-link mechanism.

TABLE 4.1
Parameters of Link Segments

Segment Description	Segment Number	Length (Meters)	Mass (Kg)	Moment of Inertia (kg.m²)
Head Section—Fixed	1	0.20	0.18	0.0072
Joint 1	2	0.10	0.07	0.0007
Joint 2	3	0.07	0.03	0.000147
Joint 3—Caudal fin	4	0.03	0.02	0.000018

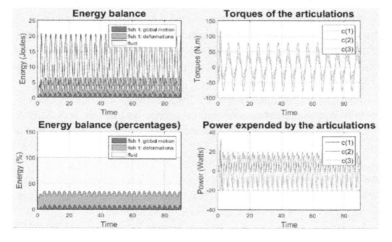

Figure 4.18   Energy distribution at three-link hinges.

TABLE 4.2
Optimal Link Fitting Using RBFM

Servo Link Distance from Head (Ratio)	Curve Fitting	
	Curve Fitting Method	Rigid Body Fitting Method
0	0.0	0.0
1.4	0.2	0.3
2.7	−0.4	0.2
3.6	−1.4	−0.9
4.4	−1.9	−1.9

from the body wave. When it is too close to be fit, the error region can be ignored. Here, linear and square values of error distribution are computed and listed in Table 4.2.

$$S_{err} = \int_{x_h}^{x_\tau} \left(y_f - y_s\right)^2 dx \qquad (4.23)$$

$$L_{err} = \int_{x_h}^{x_\tau} \left(y_f - y_s\right) dx \qquad (4.24)$$

Integral of the body wave and fitting curve is calculated using Equation 4.23. Then square error or integral of the second order derivative is calculated based on Equation 4.24 and their differences are listed in Table 4.2.

The speed of the swimming robot is also listed in Table 4.3 for varying operational frequency with respect to the relays generating body wave. Error at discrete time points are showing visible difference in terms of performance between joint curve fitting and rigid body fitting methods, as the second one has little and ignorable amount of deviation in determing the location of link segments.

TABLE 4.3

Speed Comparison with and without Optimal Link Length

Frequency in Hz	Steady-State Swimming in m/s	
	Linear Fit before Optimization	Linear Fit after Optimization
0.5	0.14	0.17
0.6	0.14	0.17
0.7	0.16	0.19
0.8	0.17	0.22
0.9	0.18	0.23
1.0	0.19	0.25
1.1	0.21	0.26
1.2	0.22	0.28
1.3	0.23	0.29
1.4	0.24	0.31
1.5	0.25	0.32

TABLE 4.4
Stiffness of Fin

Length in cm	Velocity in cm/s		
	Fin Stiffness 0.3×10^{-4} N^2	Fin Stiffness 0.5×10^{-4} Nm^2	Fin Stiffness 0.7×10^{-4} Nm^2
0.50	10	9	9
0.75	11	10	10
1.00	12	10	10
1.25	13	11	12
1.50	14	11	14
1.75	15	11	15
2.00	16	12	15
2.25	17	14	17
2.50	18	14	19
2.75	19	16	20
3.00	20	16	22

Similarly, when operating the robotic fish at varying frequencies ranging from 0.5 to 1.5Hz, it gets significant improvement in the steady-state swimming mode by generating 21% extra forward thrust.

Yet another factor influencing the efficiency of swimming fish is stiffness of material used to design fins, irrespective of modes. It's also coupled with the length of fin, and stiffness values of 0.3 and 0.7 have similar velocity, but a change of just 1 cm in length has difference in velocity of about 3 cm to 4 cm. When the stiffness value is 0.5, we could see the change in velocity is limited to only 2 cm, which can be seen from Table 4.4.

4.8 CONCLUSION

The main aim of this research work is to develop a PSO algorithm-based critical parameters affecting the efficiency of swimming robotic fish based on Lighthill and Wu's waving plate theory for oscillation and undulation. Apart from that, four natural effects of swimming fish have been identified, and they have been implemented using a mathematical model developed for both oscillatory and undulatory modes of swimming. Efficiency of fish swimming is calculated by analyzing the vortices and wakes generated from the movement of parts of the fish body and caudal fins. Moreover, we also tested the same with various fin types, such as lunated, indented, and forked. In general, caudal fin type decides the thrust and propulsive efficiency of fish with aspect ratio, heaving amplitude, and flexibility of fin material. Swimming body must compromise with either thrust or efficiency as they inversely affect each other.

In the future, this work can be enhanced by implementing a mathematical model and controller for suction-based vortices and wakes affecting the efficiency of swimming velocity with a variety of fin types and materials for multiple swimming modes. With the rigid body segments, the characteristic parameters in the simplified propulsive model of bio-mimetic robot fish were optimized based on hydrodynamic properties. The optimal link-length ratio was numerically calculated by an improved constrained cyclic variable method, and applied in BhT simulation of the three-linked robot fish.

Future research should be concentrated on multiple control parameters optimization, combining with kinematics and hydrodynamics to achieve higher propulsive speed. In the meantime, developing an optimization algorithm for autonomous navigation for robot fish based on multiple sensors fusion and intelligent control techniques will also be investigated.

REFERENCES

1. Carabineanu A. 1999. Incompressible flow past oscillatory wings of low aspect ratio by integral equations method, *International Journal of Numerical Methods in Engineering*, 45:1187–1201.
2. Carabineanu A. 2008. Self-propulsion of oscillating wings in incompressible flow, *International Journal of Numerical Methods for Fluids*, 56:1–21.
3. Yu J., Wang L. 2005. Parameter optimization of simplified propulsive model for biomimetic robot fish. *Proceedings of the IEEE International Conference on Robotics and Automation*, Barcelona, pp. 3317–3322.
4. Yu S., Ma S., Li B., Wang Y. 2009. An amphibious snakelike robot: Design and motion experiments on ground and in water. *Proceedings of the IEEE International Conference on Information and Automation*, Zhuhai/Macau, China, pp. 500–505.
5. Solanki P. B., Dutta S., Behera L. 2012. Design and 3D simulation of a robotic fish. *Proceedings of Advances in Control and Optimization of Dynamic Systems ACODS*.
6. Liu J., Hu H. 2004. A 3D simulator for autonomous robotic fish. *International Journal of Automation and Computing*, 1:42–50.

7. Webba A. P., Phillipsa C. W. G., Hudsona D. A., Turnocka S. R. 2012. Can lighthill's elongated body theory predict hydrodynamic forces in underwater undulatory swimming? *9th Conference of the International Sports Engineering Association (ISEA) 2012.*
8. Wu T. Y.-T. 1961. Swimming of a waving plate. *Journal of Fluid Mechanics*, 10:321–355.
9. Yaakob O. B., Ahmed Y. M., Said A. F. 2014. Fish locomotion for innovative marine propulsion systems. *International Journal of Biological, Biomolecular, Agricultural, Food and Biotechnological Engineering*, 8:1–5.
10. Tokic G. and Yue D. K. P. 2012. Optimal shape and motion of undulatory swimming organisms. *Proceedings of the Royal Society B, Biological Sciences.*
11. Lauder G. V., Flammang B., Alben S. 2012. Passive robotic models of propulsion by the bodies and caudal fins of fish. *Integrative and Comparative Biology*, 52:576–587.
12. Yu J., Wang L. 2005. Parameter optimization of simplified propulsive model for biomimetic robot fish. *IEEE Explore.*
13. Brad J., Colin G. S. P., Costello J. H., Dabiri J. O. 2015. Suction-based propulsion as a basis for efficient animal swimming. *Nature Communications.*
14. Xie G. 2001. An improved constrained cyclic variable method. *Journal of Fluid Mechanics*, 28:19–21.
15. Hirata K. 2016. Design and manufacturing of a small fish robot. *Processing of Japan Society for Design Engineering*, 99:29–32. https://en.wikipedia.org/wiki/Bio-inspired_robotics.
16. Korkmaz D., Koca Ozmen G., Akpolat Z. H. 2011. Robust forward speed control of a robotic fish. Sixth International Advanced Technologies Symposium, Elazig/Turkey, pp. 33–38.
17. Chowdhury A. R., Xue W., Behera M. R., Panda S. K. 2016. Hydrodynamics study of a BCF mode bioinspired robotic-fish underwater vehicle using Lighthill's slender body model. *Journal of Marine Science and Technology*, 21:102–114.
18. Homentcovschi D. 1977. Theory of lifting surface in unsteady motion in an inviscid fluid. *Acta Mechanica*, 54:221–238.
19. Ruiz L. A., Whittlesey R. W., Dabiri J. O. 2011. Vortex-enhanced propulsion. *Journal of Fluid Mechanics*, 668:5–32. Cambridge University Press.
20. Liu J., Hu H. 2004. A 3D simulator for autonomous robotic fish, *International Journal Automation and Computing*, 1:42–50.
21. Anu Priya A., Raja Mohamed S. 2016. A survey on various robotic fish models based on oscillatory motion. *International Journal of Computer Applications*, 142:37–42.
22. Swarnamugi S., Raja Mohamed S., Raviraj P. 2016. A survey on undulatory motion based robotic fish design. *Computer Applications: International Journal* 3:1–10.

23. Lighthill M. J. 1960. Note on the swimming of slender fish. *Journal of Fluid Mechanics*, 9:305–317.
24. Lighthill J. 1971. Large-amplitude elongated body theory of fish locomotion. *Proceedings of the Royal Society B, Biological Sciences*, 179:125–138.
25. Sfakiotakis M., Lane D. M., Davies J. B. C. 1999. Review of fish swimming modes for aquatic locomotion. *IEEE Journal of Oceanic Engineering*, 24:237–252.
26. Triantafyllou, M. S., Triantafyllou, G. S. 1995. An efficient swimming machine. *Scientific American*, 272:64–70.
27. Palmisano J. S., Ramamurti R., Geder J. D., Pruessner M., Sandberg W. C., Ratna B. How to maximize pectoral fin efficiency by control of flapping frequency and amplitude.
28. William H. C. C. 2015. BR3 a biologically inspired fish-like robot actuated by SMA-based artificial muscles. Ph.D Thesis, Universidad Politecnica de Madrid.
29. Barrett D., Grosenbaugh M., Triantafyllou M. 1996. The optimal control of a flexible hull robotic undersea vehicle propelled by an oscillating foil. *IEEE AUV Symposium*, 1–9.
30. Munnier A. 2009. Locomotion of deformable bodies in an ideal fluid. *Newtonian versus Lagrangian Formalisms*, 19:665–663.

INDEX

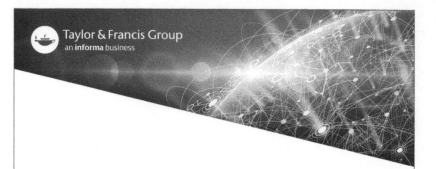